On Being a Woman

Musings of a Radical Mother

⋅⋐⋑⋅

Sharon A. Myers

Trafford
PUBLISHING

Order this book online at www.trafford.com/07-1649
or email orders@trafford.com

Most Trafford titles are also available at major online book retailers.

© Copyright 2008 Sharon A. Myers.

All rights reserved. No part of this publication may be reproduced, stored in a retrieval system, or transmitted, in any form or by any means, electronic, mechanical, photocopying, recording, or otherwise, without the written prior permission of the author.

Photographs & Illustrations: by the author

Note for Librarians: A cataloguing record for this book is available from Library and Archives Canada at www.collectionscanada.ca/amicus/index-e.html

Printed in Victoria, BC, Canada.

ISBN: 978-1-4251-4044-1

Trafford
PUBLISHING

www.trafford.com

North America & international
toll-free: 1 888 232 4444 (USA & Canada)
phone: 250 383 6864 ♦ fax: 250 383 6804
email: info@trafford.com

The United Kingdom & Europe
phone: +44 (0)1865 722 113 ♦ local rate: 0845 230 9601
facsimile: +44 (0)1865 722 868 ♦ email: info.uk@trafford.com

10 9 8 7 6 5 4 3

Thank you, Fay

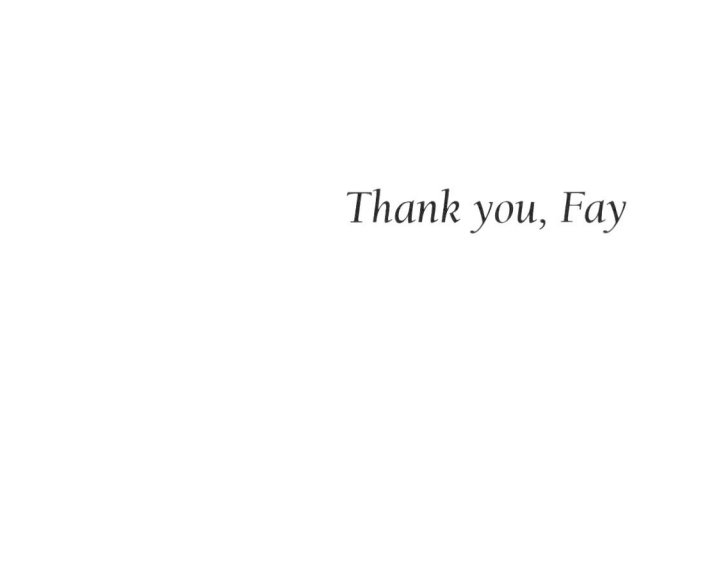

Preface and Acknowledgements

This book contains the thoughts and insights of many feminists of my generation—so many that I can no longer identify them all because I so fully absorbed their ways of seeing. (If there is any plagiarism in here, let me know, and I'll fumigate it forthwith). I am especially indebted to the great work of Nancy Chodorow, Dorothy Dinnerstein, and Sandra Harding for their pioneering analyses of the social and psychological consequences (for everybody) of mothering in a patriarchal world, and I hope to have contributed supporting insights of my own. The research of Ann Oakley and the flabbergasted humor shown in the work of Robin Morgan inspired and enabled my own investigations of the labyrinths of housework.

Most of the book was written years ago, unpublished until now due to my particular juxtaposition of the same old reasons why Tillie Olsen and countless other women have had to put aside their writing. I wrote it not as a scholarly project (I had no advanced degrees in those days), but as a synthesis of what I was learning myself about the history, economics, politics, and contradictions of being a woman. I wanted to share this knowledge with my own daughter and to share the hope it brought with it. I offer them to her here, and to other readers who might find some of these insights, or the connections among them, useful or enlightening, or both, in understanding their own lives.

I am grateful to the late Meridel Le Sueur and to Bettina Aptheker, who both took the time to read the original manuscript and to offer their advice and encouragement.

July 10, 2007
Los Angeles

Contents

	Introduction	1
I.	Origins of the Gender Order	7
II.	Childwork	37
III.	The Politics of Progress	55
IV.	The All-Powerful Female	77
V.	The All-Powerful Female from Another Angle	95
VI.	Marxists and the Shortest Revolution	105
VII.	Color: The Dispersion of Light	117
VIII.	Patriarchy and Racism: Propagating Waves	133
IX.	The Mirror Effect	151
X.	The Shitwork Factor	159
XI.	A Vision	175
	References	207
	Illustrations	209

The voice of the mother to the daughter is the rarest voice in literature.

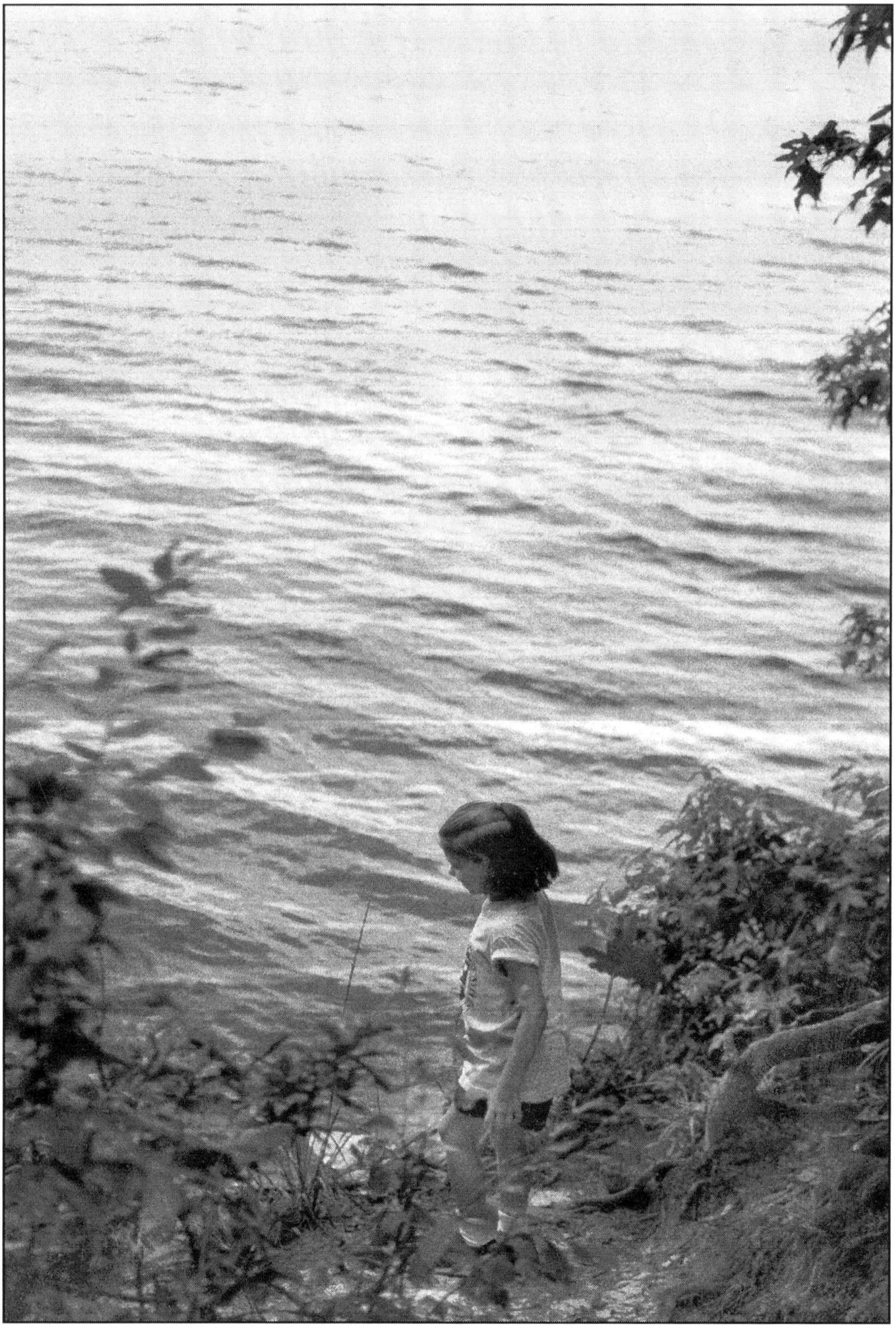

Beloved daughter,

This is your time. It's all the time you'll ever have.

You owe it to yourself.

Since you are a woman, you are surrounded with messages telling you to believe that your time is not yours because you are a woman.

·⟨≫⟩·

Your self

Your life

Your time

are the same thing. Men can't tell you about being a woman. No matter how much a man loves you, he can't comprehend what it means to experience life as a woman. Most men don't even have objective knowledge about it, not because it isn't accessible to them but because it's never been important to them.

All women can offer some survival information, but the quality of their understanding varies a lot. Feminists are a good source, but how aware they are, how they understand their dilemmas, and how they go about trying to do something about them, vary also in scope and depth, such that there are various feminisms. Feminists disagree, but they have the best information, such as it is, and the best analyses of womens' experience. As I sink into your past, displacing you into your womanhood, I feel compelled to write to the woman you are becoming because being a woman will so profoundly influence your experience of your time/life/self. I want to write to you about ideas from Nancy Chodorow, Dorothy Dinnerstein, Nawal el Saadawi, Sandra Harding, Tillie Olsen, and Evelyn Reed. These are only a few women with good insights. I want to write to you about ideas of my own.

I am hoping you won't waste any effort or life(time) trying to reinvent the wheel and figure out alone the basic knowledge all enlightened women have already discovered—and learn in time, or you'll never acquire the role of a scientist or a musician or anything other than a "woman," and you won't even realize it because you will be blithely going along, telling yourself that those dreams are not dead: they are just delayed.

Time

(Your lifetime)

is what it's all about

Feminists can help all women survive within the other circumstances of their lives, including culture, class, race, differing abilities, and sexual orientation. Within those circumstances, they can help you learn what you need to know so you can live as you decide to live and work at what you decide to work at in your life.

Your time.

Not

after you iron shirts or tidy up for daddy

after you've done the dishes

after you've grown up

after you've worried for hours about what your boyfriend

thinks of you

after you shave yourself, mutilate your feet, fry your hair,

bind your breasts, paint your face, burn your cervix with chemicals, paint your fingernails and toenails, pluck out your eyebrows, and starve yourself

after you get over the experience of being beaten or raped by men

after you've lost weight

after work (some other work)

after you've decided what to wear

after you've gotten married

after you've had a child or children

after you're not feeling so exhausted

after you've cleaned up the house

after you've gotten dinner ready

after the baby goes to sleep

after you do your "volunteer work"

after you've taken care of your husband's (or lover's) needs

after you've helped your husband's (or lover's) career (lifetime) get off the ground

after you've gotten out of the hospital, mental institution, guru's compound, self-realization seminar, unrelated college courses, battered women's shelter, welfare office, alcoholics' clinic, drug abuse clinic,

deferred dream hotels for the oppressed, many of whom, women and men alike, had no power to avoid registering in or being registered in,

where all this "womanly self-sacrifice" (time sacrifice) (life sacrifice) which is within your control also leads.

They can help you learn, insofar as your circumstances permit, how to live and work at what you decide to work at, in your time,

not

after the revolution

after every other oppressed group in the world (with men in it) achieves liberation

after you've raised a child or children

after your children are educated

after the mortgage is paid off (if you are lucky enough ever to be burdened by one)

after you've taken care of your aging parents' needs

after you've taken care of your dying husband's needs

after your life(time)

after you've been buried.

<hr />

Time

Your time

is you.

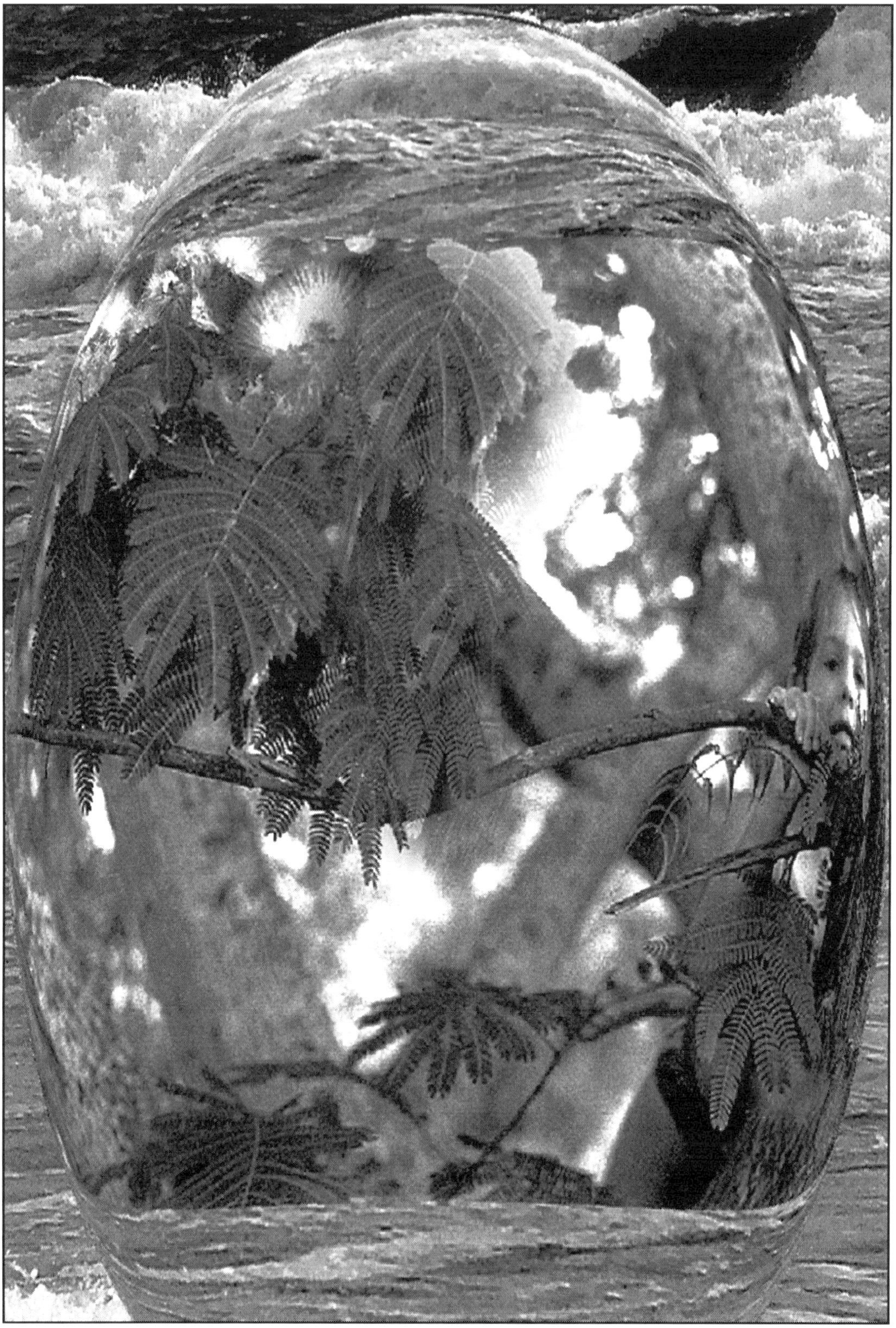

CHAPTER I

Origins of the Gender Order

Women are endowed with all the intelligence, vulnerability, beauty, and potential for transformation that men are born with. We share with men "the human condition." That is, we are conscious of the fact that we are going to die. All of the paradoxes and contradictions and mysteries and wonder and pain inherent in humanity are experiences we share with men.

In an evolutionary sense, mind and spirit (the quality of our consciousness) are what make us human. (Human as differentiated from other animals). This mind, this spirit, this consciousness, has evolved in animal bodies.

We share the animal condition with men: we eat, drink, defecate, shelter ourselves from the elements, seek to fulfill our sexual urges. As animals we share with men a great beauty. We inhabit bodies which are infinitely complex, in a planet, a galaxy, a universe of endless splendor.

Of course, at the same time, we differ at the animal level in that once human life has been created (in a petri dish or a female body), women and only women can produce it. Production takes about nine months of a woman's life(time). Once human life is produced, anybody can nourish it and keep it going until it is viable. It can be enhanced by giving it the milk we also produce for that purpose, an enhancement basically accomplished six weeks after birth.

These two functions exclusive to women, the production of human life and its special enhancement, are done—simultaneously with other life activities—in less than a year. They don't completely occupy a woman's time. She meanwhile eats, sleeps, reads books, works, argues, makes scientific discoveries, and engages in stupid behavior just as men do. The period of time that these production months are actually occupied in purely animal endeavor (birthing and suckling) related to the production process itself can actually be measured in hours.

There are a few hours in her lifetime during which she is physically incapable of attending to other human work, if she chooses to have a child or children in the first place. In this way, a woman is (if she bears children), a few hours different from a man.

There are other biological differences between women and men in, for example, average body size, weight, strength, and contour. There are differences in chemistry and architecture that reveal differences in the processing of cognitive, emotional, and linguistic information, but none of their differences preclude men or women from undertaking work performed by the other sex. Nor are the differences unmodifiable, either within individual human lifetimes or across generations, a point I will come back to toward the end of this letter.

None of the differences between women and men are significant in terms of the value of human life and work.

·⁓·

When you discover that all the differences between men and women exist on the animal plane, and that all they amount to are a few hours, and then you discover that being a woman has such overwhelming human consequences, you wonder why. And since the real difference between you and men is relatively small and exclusively animal, you keep going back to the animal to figure it out.

This is an error, as we have evolved beyond unconscious reproduction. Unlike animals, women can choose whether to exercise this extra ability or not. I think this has been true since humans made the connection between fucking and birth and women learned that if they didn't want to produce children (or any more children), the way to do it was to avoid sex with men.

And many women who wanted control of their lifetimes did indeed say no, learned to masturbate or sublimate or satisfy their sexual urges with other women: became nuns and saints and outlaws and lesbians. Some persuaded their husbands or lovers to practice primitive birth control methods (like withdrawal) or just practiced primitive birth control methods themselves (like putting a leaf in the uterus, which works on the same principle that modern and supposedly male invented intrauterine devices do). Women were just as curious about science and gifted with art and human as men were and wanted to satisfy their human urges. The fate of women (as a gender) is presently determined by human forces, not animal forces.

A sexual difference refers to the physical difference between women and men. Gender refers to the socially constructed difference between women and men. It's important to keep that in mind, because the human forces which have made womanhood such an oppressed state want you to believe that your destiny is determined by animal forces beyond your control. There is no point in getting dragged into big animal arguments about "reproductive instinct" or "maternal instinct."

Life, as Kahlil Gibran wrote, longs for itself.

It reproduces itself like crazy, it likes itself so much.

In animals it organizes a bewildering number of ways for males and females to reproduce it. Some species are organized sexually in such a fashion that the male and female mate, the female eats the male, reproduces, and goes about her business. In the depths of the ocean there's a little fish that becomes both male and female in its lifetime and reproduces itself. Apes, the primates whom we are most supposed to resemble, are organized into a loose sort of polygamy.

The point of these examples is that even at the animal level there are many ways sexuality gets organized. Life is blissfully uninterested in how sexuality is organized. Life is willing to experiment in all sorts of bizarre and breathtaking ways to take form and strut its stuff. It's even been willing to mutate whole species into and out of existence. So we don't have to worry that we are going to violate any fixed laws by controlling our life/times in such a way as to satisfy our human urges. The only fixed law in life (nature) is change. It was life that evolved us from other animals and into humanity. That seems to be the direction life "wants" us to take.

Beware of all the animal arguments about sexuality because they are all versions of an enormous lie called biological determinism. This ism can be summed up in the following (nut)shell:

Your sex is your destiny.
You reproduce so you weren't meant to do anything else.
Men don't reproduce so they are meant to do everything else.

This thinking is shattered simply looking at women such as Marie Curie, Nawal El Saadawi, Alexandra Kollontai, Audre Lorde, Sor Juana Ines de La Cruz, Ida B. Wells, Domitila Barrios de Chungara, Tatyana Ludvinskaya, Elizabeth Gurley Flynn, Rachel Carson, Granny D. Haddock, Hanan Ashrawi...

It falls down on its own terms.

Following this logic:

Men can take care of children.
So men were meant to take care of children.

Men can create nuclear weapons.
So men were meant to destroy the world.

Of course life longs for itself, longing expressed as sexual desire. This longing, this "instinct" is shared by women and men. Unlike animals, we are in control of when and how we fulfill it. There are plenty of humans on the earth. Life is not threatened by failing to produce more humans every time we have sexual contact. Life is not even threatened if individual women do not reproduce at all. Children are desirable in themselves and a great many women will always choose to have them.

Beware of all the animal arguments about sexuality because they mean that we are committing a great evil if we do not behave like animals.

Like men, we can choose sexual pleasure by masturbation; in combination with men; in combination with women. We can choose to have children when we want them, or not to have them at all. Unlike other animals, we can choose, even after production has begun, not to go on with production.

As women we are supposed to be possessed of something called a "maternal" instinct. Unlike sexual desire, this form of life's longing for itself does not manifest itself until after a child is born. After a child is born, your breasts will ache to be sucked. When they are sucked, it is a very sexy feeling. Just as a penis is engorged and needs to be relieved, or your clitoris is engorged and needs to be relieved, after you have a child your breasts will be engorged and need to be relieved. In reality, they can be relieved by anybody sucking them, or a breast pump sucking them, or by you pressing out the milk. But it is very nice indeed when a baby does it and this makes babies very happy and turns you on and enhances their immune system so even though you are perfectly well in control of this "instinct" you might as well enjoy it.

Some women choose to do this for quite a while. Some women don't do it at all, and some do it for just a few weeks. That is the extent of the "maternal instinct." The famous "maternal instinct" does not extend to a ravenous desire to change diapers and boil bottles. All the rest of the pleasures and headaches of nourishing and rearing a child can elicit the same reactions in men as they do in women. Men, too, are capable of getting all fuzzy and melted down by cuddling a baby. Men, too, get weary from sleep deprivation.

According to the "maternal instinct" version of biological determinism, you are supposed to feel some mysterious power (guilt) overtake you every time you see a baby or a child (if you don't already have a few). This mysterious power (ringing ears? Tingling skin? High blood pressure?) is supposed to give women an overwhelming desire to have and care for children. If you believe this, just try to find a babysitter.

If you believe this, find out just how badly you *want* to find a babysitter.

In fact, you have this extra ability. If you haven't chosen to have a child yet, you do look at babies curiously. You haven't yet chosen to exercise the ability and may not be sure that you even want to. Looking at babies and looking at their mothers curiously is a natural thing. Of course you are interested.

Do not mistake this curiosity for "instinct."

There's no point going back looking for animal answers, either, because the whole question of human reproduction has emerged so far out of the animal realm that it's transcending male/female relations altogether. Male and female bodies don't even need to make contact for life to be conceived. At this point the female body is still needed for production, but other means of production may be developed. We can now determine the sex of offspring at an early stage of production and choose to have them or not. Cloning, common now of plants and other animals, may well have already been done of humans. New developments in human reproduction are bringing up all sorts of human questions about human life: eugenics, fetal surgery, sperm and ovum banks, rentawombs, genetic engineering (planned races? underclasses of drones? female populations solely for male sexual pleasure?), "genetic counseling." All of these issues have consequences far beyond physical reproduction. There is no point in looking at other animals for the answers to gender oppression.

Sociobiologists speculate that much of human sexual behavior is conditioned by our genetic history. That is, that at a level not determined by consciousness, but by genetic tendency, men tend to seek many sexual partners because it enhances the likelihood that their genes will survive, while women are more sparing and choosy about their sexual partners because, unlike men, they cannot spread their genes around indiscriminately; they can have only a limited number of children in their lifetimes. So, according to this interpretation of human behavior, typical female behavior is to seek stable partnerships which will enhance the likelihood that the children they do have (and will propagate their genes) will survive. In accordance with this theory, sociobiologists speculate, for example, that men are sexually attracted to young women because young women are more likely to propagate their genes; to women with small waists because that signals the woman is not already pregnant; to women with curvaceous hips because (whether accurate or not), they seem to signal the capacity to bear children.

I think our evolutionary history has undoubtedly predisposed us toward certain behaviors. Note, however, that a predisposition is not a fixed law. As Dawkins says, "There is no reason why the influence of genes cannot easily be reversed by other influences" (268).

Genetically we seem to be predisposed to like fatty foods and sweet foods, too, but we have to overcome such preferences in the modern world. The 'fight or flight' response to stress which may have served us well in earlier environments is not so useful in modern urban life and may lead to hypertension and other ills. Our cultural evolution has far outstripped our physical evolution.

Oppression of women comes from a human organization of human survival. The organization is (and has been for a long time extending into prehistory) based on a system called patriarchy.

Patriarchy is a system of power relations.

This system of power relations emerges out of a human division of the labor necessary to human survival in which:

1. *the production of socialized humans* (humans who will reproduce the organization necessary to human survival);

2. *the production of self-esteem* necessary to human survival (the servicing of all human emotional needs unprovided for in the social relations of the production of the material goods and services necessary to human survival);

3. *the production of most of the leisure time* historically necessary for the development of the means of the production of the material goods and services necessary to human survival (now primarily utilized by men for personal consumption); and

4. *the production of all goods and services not profitable or surplus-producing* (goods and services usually for immediate consumption) necessary for human survival

are produced exclusively by one category of humans:

women,

so that another category of humans (men) can attend to the production of the material goods and services necessary to human survival which produce surplus or profit, if they work at all. (Although this work is not done exclusively by men, men work almost exclusively in this area of the organization).

In addition to doing all the labor performed exclusively by women, women participate in the labor system which does produce profit or surplus when their services in that system are (in reality) or are construed to be, in the interests of men.

In this system, men have more power (energy) than women.

Women have less power, not only because they receive far fewer material and emotional rewards than men do, but because they are exhausted by this system.

Forcibly then, patriarchy is a system of male dominance and female submission. It is this system, this power relationship, which oppresses women and aims to rob you of your time (your lifetime).

We need to understand patriarchy and empower ourselves to change it, because the socialization of men in these ways has dehumanized men, who, by doing human work in the context of these power relations, have made an appalling mess of the world. And if allowed to continue being socialized in and working in these power relations, men have the power now to make an even more, inconceivably more appalling mess out of the world than they already have, if they don't destroy us all first.

The division of labor which led to patriarchy originated far back in prehistory and was indeed a function of the animal difference between women and men, but its development into the system of patriarchy was a strictly human affair.

The earliest human groups we have evidence of were small groups who foraged for food or survived by some combination of foraging and hunting. This was the longest of all the periods of our survival as humans, compared to all the periods which followed it. There is some evidence that it extends back as far as three million years. During this period, patriarchy did not necessarily exist.

Of course, it isn't safe to assume that things were equally tough for humans everywhere all of the time, but it must have been very tough for a very long time, because for a very long time there is only evidence of humans in these small groups. There is no evidence of large populations of them existing together anywhere until a time which is very late relative to how long we have evidence of human existence.

I would like to speculate about these small, mobile groups of humans existing by some combination of foraging and hunting for food in tough conditions. By tough conditions, I mean that there was no reliable surplus of food. There might have been windfalls now and then of extra food, but not a surplus that could be counted on. This kind of economy is basically the same that all animals live in, and with small variation, it seems to be the one humans lived in for the longest period of our existence.

There was no birth control and women probably got pregnant frequently.

But given the tough conditions as well as human ignorance, it is safe to assume that there was a high attrition rate among babies who did manage to get born,

so that at any given time women were not likely to have been burdened by more than one before a surviving baby was mobile enough to forage, too, or at least follow along. So, even though there was no birth control, women were probably not burdened down with a lot of infants. Nor were they burdened down with caring for the sick and the aged, as neither survived. There were no houses to clean and what little refuse there was was excreted or put outside of such shelter as existed. Much of the work which patriarchy now forces upon women did not exist. Both men and women spent their lifetimes occupied in essentially the same endeavors, with the exception of feeding children, which simply required of women greater animal endurance, which women indeed developed.

With no predictable surplus time, food, or energy, it often must have taken most of the resources at the command of each individual to survive. I think there are some things that we can safely speculate about in such economies. Under tough conditions, the division of labor between women and men would have been relatively small. Women, like men, had to hunt and forage; had to defend themselves from the elements and from predators; had to be mobile. No one would have had a lot of leisure time.

Women had babies and since women produced milk for them, the only way babies could survive was by close proximity to their mothers, at least until they developed teeth. So, in addition to hunting and foraging, women had this extra weight to move around and also, for considerable periods, the appetite of women was greater than the appetite of men, relative to their weight.

I think it's likely that under those tough conditions, where women had to do all the same things men did to get food, and where women had this extra six to twenty pounds to carry and another 400 calories or so to scare up daily, that women had to develop a very high degree of endurance (not brute physical strength, but endurance). And that that period was so long that the development of that extra endurance expresses itself biologically today in the fact that women live longer than men (a state of affairs which seems subsequently to be maintained by purely cultural factors).

Some women, in despair over the behavior of men, have postulated the origin of patriarchy in the larger size of men and in rape, so I want to stop and examine this sad hypothesis: it's another version of biological determinism.

The muscular development of humans so occupied was great. Women had powerful, muscular bodies. Even today, in agricultural communities where both sexes labor side by side, under equally brutal conditions, year after year (and I have seen this in remote Andean valleys where there were no roads connecting communities to larger markets, and where bronze age means of production and culture were largely intact), it can be observed that there is remarkably little difference between male and female bodies, in either stature or mass, compared to the differences between women and men in more affluent economies. The only sizable physical difference is the large lump located on women's backs.

Also, women could not have doubted their muscular abilities. They could see, day in and day out, that they were quite strong. Women have one physical advantage over men when it comes to rape, which is the vulnerable and exposed state of male genitals. There is no reason to suppose that any conditioning existed in those women to prevent them from using that advantage, or, given the psychology of rapists, who look for helplessness and the assurance of a lack of negative consequences for themselves before engaging in rape, to imagine that such women were inviting targets for it. Or to assume that men who spent their entire lifetimes in an often exhausting struggle to preserve their lives and their physical integrity, had the leisure time, the extra energy, or the inclination to seek pain or the possible injury of their one reliable source of pleasure by mixing it up with those athletic prehistoric women.

Then the argument goes, but what about their "weakened condition at childbearing." But look at women who work in fields, who are well developed physically by lifetimes of hard physical labor, who stop their work, birth their babies, rest a few hours or a few days, and resume working. Pregnancy in itself does not weaken women. So now we get to labor itself. The idea of some man waiting for this rare opportunity to rape a woman (and rape is an act of humiliation, not of sexual desire)—to overcome a woman who is clearly in the control of a power far greater than himself—is farfetched and certainly not the sort of thing societies get organized around.

Another thing to remember is that these were small groups of humans, exposed daily to many dangers. It would manifestly not be in a man's interest to go around humiliating someone whose failure to warn him of something could cost him his life at any moment. Rape is a socially conditioned behavior. It is a result, not a cause, of human social organization.

And while we are back in the tough times of the small groups scrabbling to make it, there is another important factor: men and women have always esteemed one another for the sexual pleasure they can afford one another. Women have always longed for sex and the idea that sex depletes energy is a patriarchal myth of the first order.

After a hard day of grubbing for roots, being manipulated by the exasperating behavior of lizards, picking thorns out of the skin, getting scratched up collecting berries, mobilizing the body over distances in search of water or away from excesses of it; a day full of real and imagined dangers, subject to every bizarre whim of nature from ants to quicksand, not to mention the known intentions of larger mammals, it is much more likely that both women and men anticipated each other's animal warmth: the pleasure, comfort, and regenerative power of sex with each other. It was the only predictable pleasure around.

Even today, in this later world where patriarchy flourishes, when the times are tough, gender elaborations tend to evaporate. Women fight. Men cry.

Those were tough times.

And when they died of broken bones no one could set; when they stumbled into a bee swarm and died of stings; when they drowned or burned or bled to death,

They keened one another.

·⊱⊰·

It is such a weary patriarchal lie that we bludgeoned each other into humanity, designed to legitimate the male-dominated institutions bludgeoning us out of it. This "male aggression/rape" theory of history is one of the most vicious forms of BD (biological determinism), because it reinforces a deep fear in the hearts of men

that it might indeed be true.

And if this is the case,

the real humanity in them

can take no other course but self-destruction.

·⊱⊰·

There was another factor present at this stage of human development that there wasn't a lot of time to elaborate on but which was, and still is, an important factor in the relations between men and women. Men feared women.

This extra ability we have which differs us from men at the animal level is pretty amazing. In reality of course, it is no different than what female grasshoppers do or what female giraffes do, but when human beings witness it in human life, it seems very awesome indeed, because it produces (wonder of wonders) human beings. And men are really awed by it because it produces (wonder of wonders) men (real humans).

Men might have been confused about the humanity of women, but they have never been confused about their own.

·⊱⊰·

Try to put yourself in the calloused feet of one of these early men, and look at women. At this time humans had not made the connection between fucking (which happened frequently), and the widely spaced event of birth. A woman, by some miraculous process, "grew" you and expelled you outside of herself. You saw women suckling male babies and knew that you had depended on women for your very existence even after your birth.

In some way unknown to you, women "created" you, and you, who are the center of the universe, know how important you are and what an amazing being you are, and know that whatever "created" you must be pretty awesome indeed.

Anybody who "creates" you, has a lot of power. You don't mess around with that kind of power, for if it was so great it could create you, it could certainly eliminate you as well.

You also knew that the red liquid in you was life. That losing that liquid meant losing your life. And yet you observed that women had so much of that powerful life stuff, were so full of it, that excesses of it oozed out of them regularly, without interfering with their lives at all.

You may even have observed, eventually, that this excess life blood flowed out of women with a regularity connected to the heavens, evidence of some powerful connections with the Big Forces which you did not have.

You could not look at these dramatic functions of the bodies of women without comparing them to your own. And what you had was a vulnerable appendage which, while it gave you deep pleasure and was highly esteemed by you for that reason, did not "do" anything except go up and down, up and down and produced a small amount of some juice which was neither a food source nor evidence of life (blood), and what is more it was capricious in this little up and down activity it manifested, revealing your innermost feelings for all to see even if you wished to conceal them.

Men did not know how important they were to the dramatic reproductive functions they observed in women.

⁂

Now, all humans have to feel self-esteem. Self-esteem is necessary to human survival. In the absence of it, humans commit suicide. And I think that it is possible that even in those early days when there wasn't much time to elaborate on social relations, it is possible that men felt impelled to acts of prowess in the physical activities they did engage in, and that they very well may have pushed themselves to get some extra lizards or some extra berries and even offered them to the women in an effort to prove to themselves and prove to the women

that they were powerful, too.

Men are still doing this.

I further speculate that women, who like all humans need to feel self-esteem, were very impressed by their "awesome" power themselves, just as proud of it as the men were envious (and mind you, this "envy" was not for the functions themselves, but of the power they seemed to represent), and that women probably viewed the extraneous antics of men with the same condescending attitude they do today:

knew, as women know today,

that men needed to feel important;

that men are unendurable and destructive when they do not;

and even though women did not and could not depend exclusively on men in such economies, when you are compelled to get so many extra calories a day under such conditions,

an extra lizard is an extra lizard.

Women probably did reward such offerings as men could come up with in those economies, with the esteem men sought.

Who had power in these gritty economies?

Nature.

Physically, women and men were equally equipped to deal with it, with women holding a slight edge over men in endurance, men in brute strength, but psychologically, the Big Power (the force of nature) was attributed to women.

As time went on, in many places, the division of labor in these small groups foraging for plants, fruit, roots, grubs, and bird eggs was widened (probably in conjunction with the control of fire), with women foraging over an area closer to camp and men ranging out farther in search of ever larger animals.

This further division of labor could only have brought prestige to the successful hunters, and solidified and enhanced the prestige of women, because foraging is a much more reliable supply of food than hunting. Men who came back empty-handed could still eat, as could the women and children. In the last analysis, the hunting economy, whether backed up by foraging or later, subsistence agriculture, depended on the labor of women.

Evelyn Reed, who pointed this out in *Problems of Women's Liberation*, analyzed the consequences of this widening division of labor in the production of the material goods and services necessary to human survival, tracing the development of surplus-producing industries to the labor of women. One of the greatest of these was agriculture, as women turned up and aerated the earth with their digging sticks, observing and eventually controlling the processes of plant growth. I think it is possible that they measured time and growing cycles by the lunar coincidence of menstruation.

In foraging and hunting small animals, women also are likely to have begun domesticating animals. Today, in the Andes, small rodents called "cui" are cultivated by women in the huts of Quechua speaking people and in some areas are the chief source of animal protein. I mention this because we are so accustomed to thinking exclusively of larger mammals as "domesticated."

The need for food storage was especially compelling for women, who chew and process food for babies whose stomachs are small and whose need for food is correspondingly more frequent than the need of adults.

Reed documents the development of food preparation and storage by women; the production of equipment (pottery, utensils, ovens, storage houses) necessary for such preparation and storage; the development of techniques to remove poisonous substances in food; the discovery and control of medicinal properties in plant and animal substances; the development of the use of animal byproducts, leather, cordage, tanning; the processing and weaving of grass fibers and bark; of weaving and the development of textiles; of architecture and engineering in the construction of dwellings (here she quotes Briffault):

> We are no more accustomed to think of the building art and of architecture than of boot-making or the manufacture of earthen-ware as feminine occupations. Yet the huts of the Australian, of the Andaman Islanders, of the Patagonians, of the Botocudos; the rough shelters of the Seri, the skin lodges and wigwams of the American Indians, the black camelhair tent of the Bedouin, the 'yurta' of the nomads of Central Asia are all the exclusive work and special care of the women. (41-42)

In hunting, she notes, men had to develop a certain degree of cooperative behavior among themselves, but much of hunting is still solitary, competitive labor reduced to the animal laws of predator and prey:

> So long as hunting was an indispensable full-time occupation, it relegated men to a backward existence. Hunting trips removed men for extended periods of time from the community centers and from participation in the higher forms of labor.
>
> The discovery of agriculture by the women, and their domestication of cattle and other large animals, brought about the emancipation of the men from their hunting life. Hunting was then reduced to a sport, and men were freed for education and training in the industrial and cultural life of the communities…
> In the first period of their emancipation, the work of the men, compared with that of the women, was, quite naturally, unskilled labor. They cleared away the brush and prepared the ground for cultivation by the women. They felled trees, and furnished the timber for construction work. (46)

The development of social relations following the development of surplus food supplies and the ever more sophisticated industries among women were of another order than hunting, not only because of the degree of organization inherent in the industries themselves, but because, simultaneously, women were the primary childworkers.

In the very early human societies, there is evidence that goddesses, not only gods, were important projections of human awe of and uncertainty about nature. Myths and echoes of these goddesses survive down the ages and into the present. "Nature," even today, is referred to as "Mother."

The earliest means of reckoning kinship were matrilineal, as the mothers of children could be identified with certainty but not the fathers.

Echoes of this long period are found even today in matrilineal systems. Some feminists call this the "matriarchy," but I think that is too confusing, because it implies that conditions were the reverse of what they are today, with women "over" men, which was most unlikely. I think, rather, that during this period, social relations did not entail systematic oppression of either men or women.

This order of things ended with a diminishment of the importance of female goddesses and their replacement with male images. The menstrual blood offered on the altars was replaced with the blood of other animals and the blood of human sacrifices.

It seems that that the earlier "matriarchal" order did not fall without an immense and extended struggle, because when you look at patriarchy today and you see the enormous power of its institutions, all the stunning range and strength of the legal, extra-legal, and psychological devices used to maintain it, be minded, as Nawal El Saadawi minds:

> "...the potential force that lies within a being itself decides the counter-force required to hold him or her down and to supress their capacity for resistance" (100).

She wrote this in reference to patriarchy as it is expressed in Islamic fundamentalism, but it is metaphorically accurate in many dimensions of Western cultures as well:

> The tendency among males to harm any woman caught crossing the boundaries of her home, and therefore the outer limits of the world prescribed for her by men, or who dares break into and walk through domains reserved for men, proves that they cannot consider her as merely weak and passive. On the contrary, they look upon her as a dangerous aggressor the moment she steps over the frontiers, an aggressor to be punished and made to return immediately to the restrictions of her abode. This attitude bears within itself the proof of woman's strength, a strength from which man seeks to protect himself by all possible means. Not only does he imprison woman within the house, but he also surrounds the male world with all sorts of barricades... (146)

Be minded that all the power of patriarchy is a measure of your strength, a measure of how much it takes to keep you down

and when you observe all of the fantastic mechanisms maintained to limit your sexuality; to limit your human power,

to sustain the patriarchal double standard by which men may enjoy sex at will, but women must be confined or punished—and this machinery is fabulously complex; it is still in place despite the recent illusory "sexual liberation" freeing women to be sexually exploited by many men rather than one,

from physical clitoridectomy in the east

to psychological clitoridectomy in the west

from the mutilation of bound feet

to the mutilation of high heels

be minded, daughter,

of the enormity of your human power,

of Nawal El Saadawi's insight:

That these are objective measures

designed to suppress an objective force.

❦

Evelyn Reed's analysis of gender oppression led her to believe that "As social production came into the hands of the men, women were dispossessed from productive life and driven back to their biological function of maternity. Men took over the reins of society and founded a new social system which served their needs" (47).

I think this is a very strange conclusion. Women have never been "dispossessed from productive life." They have always been extremely productive. Nor have they ever been "driven back" to their "biological function" of maternity. The "biological function" has always been with us. It is simply an extra ability.

But indeed the old order was overthrown, and indeed, "Men took over the reins of society and founded a new social system."

Reed doesn't explain how it was that men did this.

How did it fall?

I think it's simple to see how it happened.

❦

Patriarchy emerged out of the division of the labor between women and men in the long struggle for human survival impelled by two conditions: a surplus of food, and the discovery of the connection between fucking and reproduction.

Surplus food was by far the most important of the two. Patriarchy could (and did) emerge out of a surplus of food alone. By a surplus of food, I don't mean just a big windfall, like a bunch of anchovies caught in a natural harbor, or a few good years of abundant game and good luck, but a steady, predictable surplus, generation after generation.

Food surpluses came about in a number of different ways, in different times and places, and were not always the result of the development of agriculture. Surpluses could be produced by favorable climatic conditions over a long span of time creating geographical areas (such as some Pacific islands), where fruit and fish so abound all year that sophisticated means of production are unnecessary for human survival. Or by the development of food storage (such as that enabled by the drying of fish abundant in the waters of the Pacific Northwest). Or by the development of domesticated animals, or by agriculture, or by any combination of those developments.

It is the surplus itself which impels patriarchy, not some other cultural factor, and that's why all cultures, even the most so-called "primitive" ones in existence at the time history began to be recorded, were patriarchal or patriarchal to some degree, a fact which often mystifies feminists because such cultures are so diverse, they hardly seem to have anything in common from which to deduce the origins of patriarchy.

Their very existence is that common factor; for by that time, those cultures with even a small amount of predictable surplus food were the only ones left. They were the survivors in the long struggle for human survival

---

Let's go back and look at the mother of a baby in the hard scrabble times of foraging: she might put the baby down and grub hard for some roots somewhere. She knows the baby is in danger but she also knows that neither one of them will survive if she doesn't produce food and so she does the best she can to divide her consciousness between the baby and the work at hand.

She gets into it, working as hard as she can, and a rodent attacks the baby. Or the baby manages to get that interesting twig into her mouth and silently chokes to death. A lot of babies probably died of unavoidable neglect in those tough early economies. But when there is a surplus, when ignoring the baby is not a matter of life and death for the mother, when food is easier to come by and when its availability is predictable, the baby is far less likely to be ignored.

This led to the survival of a lot more babies.

And when there were a lot more babies,

it took a lot more time

(and time is what it's all about)

to take care of them.

The nurturing of babies was assumed to be the responsibility of women, an assumption based on the observation that women produced milk for them, an assumption which women probably shared themselves.

With the surplus of food

there was a surplus of babies

and the small division of labor which had formerly existed between women and men

underwent a long quantitative and qualitative change of enormous significance,

as did, consequently, the social relations between women and men.

This change in social relations took the form of gender elaboration, which came progressively under the control of the men, for whom the food surplus produced not only a change in the nature of their labor, but surplus time.

And men threw up and out of themselves all sorts of taboos and rituals and runarounds the women to feel that they could:

1) control or at least contain the women's "awesome" power

2) assure themselves of their importance and

3) assure the women of their (the men's) importance

And women, over a long time, succumbed to these taboos dippity doos definitions of their sex

1) because they were so impressed with it themselves

2) they needed and wanted the men to feel important and

3) they didn't have the *time* to do much about it one way or another, because the few hours of (real) difference with men were extended into entire life(times) of having, nourishing, and caring for children who, since there was no birth control, appeared one right after another.

And as time went on, men, who were not exhausted by this endlessly regenerative productive labor *in addition* to the production of the material goods required for human survival

had the time

(and time is what it's all about)

to get themselves a little extra knowledge.

Knowledge is power.

⁙

In the long period of the old order, as the surpluses led to ever more stable and growing populations, communities were developed along collective lines. Land was shared as community property; there were community ovens and granaries. Children were more or less a community responsibility, the work of a large extended family that was reckoned through the mother and the mother's brothers.

Evelyn Reed points out that the destruction of the old order also disintegrated the social relations of the men among themselves, the "fratriarchy," or brotherhood of men, which was composed of the men of the mother-brother clan, the matriarchal gens. Father families did not exist.

> When the European conquerors came over to this country looking for gold and met the aborigines living there, neither side could understand the outlook, customs, and standards of the other; they spoke different "social" languages. For example, when Father Le Jeune asked an Iroquois Indian how he could be so fond of children which admittedly were not his own, "the Indian looked at him contemptuously and replied: 'Thou hast no sense. You...love only your own children; we love all the children of the tribe....We are all father and mother to them. (22-23)

But all the women being mothers to them and all the men being (even good) fathers to them is quite a different thing than all the men being mothers to them and all the women being fathers to them.

Women were the primary caretakers of children.

When women emancipated men into the social relations of production made possible by the surplus of food, they neither relinquished this primary responsibility nor was it sought by the men.

Nowhere in the world, at any stage of economic survival, did a gender elaboration get elaborated in which men regularly cooked for and cleaned up after women and children. Even in the so-called "collective" days of matrilineal kin organization, all labor was not truly collective and never has been.

The internal stresses in the labor arrangement in which women monopolize childhood had to have been present in early times, even if not so developed as surplus economic conditions later allowed. I think it's safe to speculate that in economies in which men ranged out hunting while women developed collective industries in a more bounded geographic space, little boys were probably more difficult to socialize into those industries, as they longed to join the hunt with the men, chafing to claim their manhood in "male" endeavor.

Health improved. The now surviving sick and injured were deposited into the dwellings and the care of the women. Lifetimes lengthened. There was more food to enable more women to live, live longer, and produce more children.

Now, there is a threshold somewhere in childwork which has never been precisely located but exists, whereby more individual attention to individual children enhances their ability to survive, not only as animals, but as humans. (Beyond that threshold, individual attention is counter-productive).

It is easy to see how this operates by comparing the foraging mother who forcibly neglects her infant to a mother in a surplus producing economy, but more difficult to measure after that. Children are not just static creatures who need to be "cared" for like cattle. They're demanding and absorbing of all the conscious energy (work) that they can command.

   And command they do.

The need to educate them into human society becomes more work just as society becomes more complex. The children have to be taught to defend themselves (from fire, from water which now boils and steams, from poisonous plants); education is needed to protect human labor from their exuberance (to keep them from tangling the thread in the loom, disturbing the freshly planted seeds, breaking pots).

They had to be socialized into the increasingly complex social relations of gender and clan.

As communities developed and more women shared their child knowledge and child observation, a body of knowledge concerning their care and cultivation emerged which was in itself one of the great tasks of all women to learn, and which further empowered the survival of more children.

·❧·

   In short, not only were there many more children, but the process of "reproduction," producing socialized humans who will reproduce the organization necessary to human survival, became, simultaneously, more complex and time-consuming as that organization became more complex.

I think that for the majority of the children who have ever been born, even up to today, the threshold of individual attention which would enhance their survival as humans has never been crossed. That, in fact, most children do not and never have received all of the individual attention they could still benefit by.

Today, as men and women struggle to live, parents (and especially the women, who do most of the work with children and who are therefore the most sensitive to their needs) experience a painful awareness of this fact.

Back in the past, with whole communities involved in the industries which kept them alive (because it was tough then; not as tough as foraging, but tough), the refusal of a child's invitation to play, of a child's question, of an obvious learning opportunity with a child, probably wrenched the same passing emotion in the men going off to the hunt and the woman to her leather-scraping as it does today.

(In fact, in many cultures children were and still are swaddled into paralysis for a long time, so that they can be hung up somewhere or manipulated conveniently to enable women to attend to other important work).

Children need individual attention. Almost universally, they would benefit from more than they can get. They never stop trying to get it. They are intelligent, vocal creatures with sophisticated pattern recognition abilities, memories, and emotions.

In the absence of men,

in the presence of a social structure which obligates women to be their primary caretakers,

the brunt of this pressure

and it is heavy pressure

is brought to bear against the conscious

and unconscious

minds of women.

When women emancipated men into the social relations of modern production, men did not assume a correspondingly responsible role in the labor of reproduction, because that was, in the minds of women and men alike, the primary responsibility of women.

The very closeness of the early years of breastfeeding, as the woman forcibly observes the rhythms of a child's development, gives her a competence to percieve, anticipate, and respond to a child's needs which is superior to that of a man's.

Men even today observe this competence and feel inferior to women in this labor.

What clearer proof can there be that this is "women's work"?

They do it better.

Men neither sought increased responsibility in this labor nor were they obligated to assume it.

Men brought their power and their genius to the new productive industries, applying both to them most fruitfully, inventing means to ever greater surpluses and being drawn ever further into the social relations created by the very existence of those surpluses,

with no countervailing force in the organization of human survival to impede their absorption into those processes,

or, in the case of women, no force to liberate them from the increasing weight of the labor to socialize humans into those processes.

 Over time, the cumulative weight of this labor, the cumulative weight of billions of little decisions

 in favor of the increasing burden of the socialization of children,

 in favor of the demands of the children themselves,

 decisions made possible by the existence of the very surpluses women had been instrumental in creating,

 sank into the life

 times

 of women,

displacing the balance of labor which had created the now overflowing surpluses.

⁂

These changes did not come about everywhere in the same degree at the same time, and the gender elaborations which got elaborated were amazingly diverse, but the general tendency,

the accumulation of power by men

and the subjugation of women

was inexorable

and deeply aggravated by the effects of the internal laws of socialization subject to this lopsided division of labor, which we will examine a little further on.

⁂

The "matriarchy" did not fall because men had the strength to push it over.

It did not fall because women were lacking in the ability to devise surpluses.

The old order did not succumb to men.

It succumbed to babies,

to children,

to the sick and injured,

to the aged,

to life itself.

It collapsed from the weight of its own production.

⁂

The surpluses created by nature in favorable geographic circumstances, or the surpluses created by food storage alone, or even agriculture for a long time, were enough to maintain substantially greater populations of humans in a given area, but they were marginal surpluses subject to the same kind of ecological limitations that define the existence of other living organizations in a given area, such as ant colonies.

And while such populations evolved elaborate cultural forms and many of them maintained harmonious relationships with their surrounding environments which permitted their sustained existence right up to recent history,

the development of other kinds of surpluses was not always so smooth

because there is some quantitative point at which the surpluses themselves create an explosive qualitative change in all the power (energy) relations in the successively larger environments where they are produced.

The laws which govern this phenomenon are the laws

of energy.

A surplus is a concentrated form of energy.

In this sense, money is energy.

In Mesoamerica, for instance, corn surpluses facilitated the blossoming of large populations and elaborate civilizations, though they collapsed with dramatic suddenness.

Humans are still wrestling with the laws of energy which govern the surpluses they are so desirous of producing.

In fact, the production of the surpluses so deeply affecting human survival is based on the labor of women,

who produce socialized humans

(the means of the means of production)

and although women everywhere have, in addition to providing this base, participated (differentially, in different stages and forms of surplus producing economies) in the direct production of these surpluses, the patriarchal division of labor has come to exclude women from control over them.

In surplus economies, men have more time than women.

In some areas (possibly those areas where there was "natural" abundance year round), men utilized this time for personal consumption

or for the development of religions to justify or reinforce their increasing control over what surplus energy there was

or for the investigation and development of knowledge which was very advanced, but not directly related to producing more surplus or not directly applicable to producing more surplus at that stage of economic development.

But in other areas (possibly those areas where the surplus was harder to come by or less predictable or where there was a fortuitous supply of certain natural resources lending themselves to beneficial accidents)

men used that time to devise ever more advanced methods of producing surpluses.

More advanced methods are methods which produce, in addition to more food and better shelter, more time.

By producing more time, they could study and reflect and experiment and thus get even more knowledge, which led to ever greater degrees of

> power
>
> over their lives
>
> and incidentally,
>
> over the lives of women and children.

⁓⊛⁓

Somewhere along this developmental line, in all of the economies where there was more than a marginal surplus, and even in some of the economies where there was not, the connection was made between fucking and birth.

This deeply reinforced the emerging rationalizations for what was already going on. Men discovered that they had something to do with it, after all. Men discovered that they fathered children. And men now had the power to decide that the children, therefore, belonged to them—were their property, part of "their" surplus. And since women were the vehicles through which "their" property got produced, women were their property, too.

Men began attributing to themselves

the Big Power

they formerly attributed to women.

(This took some very pathetic forms, like the creation myth of a male god creating a female out of a male sparerib).

Women, whose identity was increasingly being defined primarily by the animal function of reproduction, an identity which had at least the attributes and dignity perceived in wild animals, were now seen as owned animals.

Cattle.

And as advances in human knowledge were made, permitting ever more advanced means of production for sustaining and increasing the surpluses, the role of Woman (her social relation to men) became that of an ever more

domesticated

animal.

·ᥫ᭡ᥬ·

Differentially, as the means of production kept advancing, the work that men were doing increasingly became exclusively human work, work performed with ever more sophisticated tools (from stone arrowheads to bronze blades in plows, to iron and then steel; from dugout canoes to sailing ships to aircraft carriers to space rockets). Much work that men were doing became more exclusively human in the sense that it contributed to life(times) ever more remote from the lives of other animals.

The time to do things other than survive was dedicated to purely human endeavors: science, religion, art, war, and lolling around.

Meanwhile, the work that the women were doing, in addition to maintaining this entire organization by reproducing it via the socialization of children,

and tending to all of its emotional necessities unfulfilled in the social relations of the work that men exclusively did although it was not exclusively done by men and directly laboring in the surplus material production when it was in the interest of men,

was basically animal maintenance work.

The few hours of real (animal) difference between women and men came to be extrapolated into lifetimes of childbearing, childrearing, washing, cleaning, food preparation and storage, care of the aged and sick;

were extrapolated culturally so far that it meant that women took care of all the realms of life in which men did not want to engage, all forms of non-profitable shitwork, including woman's role as man's conscience (the least profitable relation of them all).

The view of women as animals (non-human) came to be in great measure a self-fulfilling prophecy in the visible (to men) work assigned to women by the patriarchal division of labor.

The women were so busy with animal maintenance work throughout their life(times) that they did not become educated with the forms of human knowledge en(gendered) by the work and leisure of men without extreme effort or luck, or both. And even the few who did, after intense struggles, were so excluded from all but the butt end of the social relations of those activities that it was impossible to use such knowledge except in very limited ways, if at all.

Forcibly, women were never divorced from "animal" work.

Now, humans are both human (differentiated from animals by the quality of our consciousness) and animal (not differentiated from other animals). We are both human and animal and as such we have both human needs and animal needs which require work to fulfill. In reality, these needs are intertwined and deeply related to each other. In reality, all "purely human" work depends absolutely on the fulfillment of animal maintenance work first. In this sense, even the visible work which has come to be identified with women is more important than the work which has come to be identified with men, no matter how much men trivialize "women's work."

Women have always known this.

Women have been human all along and known that without their labor, men and their achievements would not even exist. It is a great "private" joke among women, which underlies a humor that springs up when women are with each other, unobserved by men.

They share a knowledge (derived from their work) which puts human achievements in a realistic perspective which men rarely have and which they badly need, for being human is deeply woven with being animal and if human work is divorced from the animal perspective, it becomes

non-human.

It becomes monstrous.

Contrary to Reed's conclusion, women were not "dispossessed from productive life." Women have only been dispossessed, in varying degrees, from many of the rewards of "productive life."

Reed's assertion also overlooked every coat ever mended, every sock ever darned, every meal ever prepared, every quilt ever labored over, every herb gathered, every fruit preserved, every sausage stuffed, every fiber washed,

every song ever sung by women.

It ignores the stunning productivity of women, the record of their *unpaid* "socially useful labor activity."

As to "being driven back to their biological function of maternity,"

The biological function is the least of it.

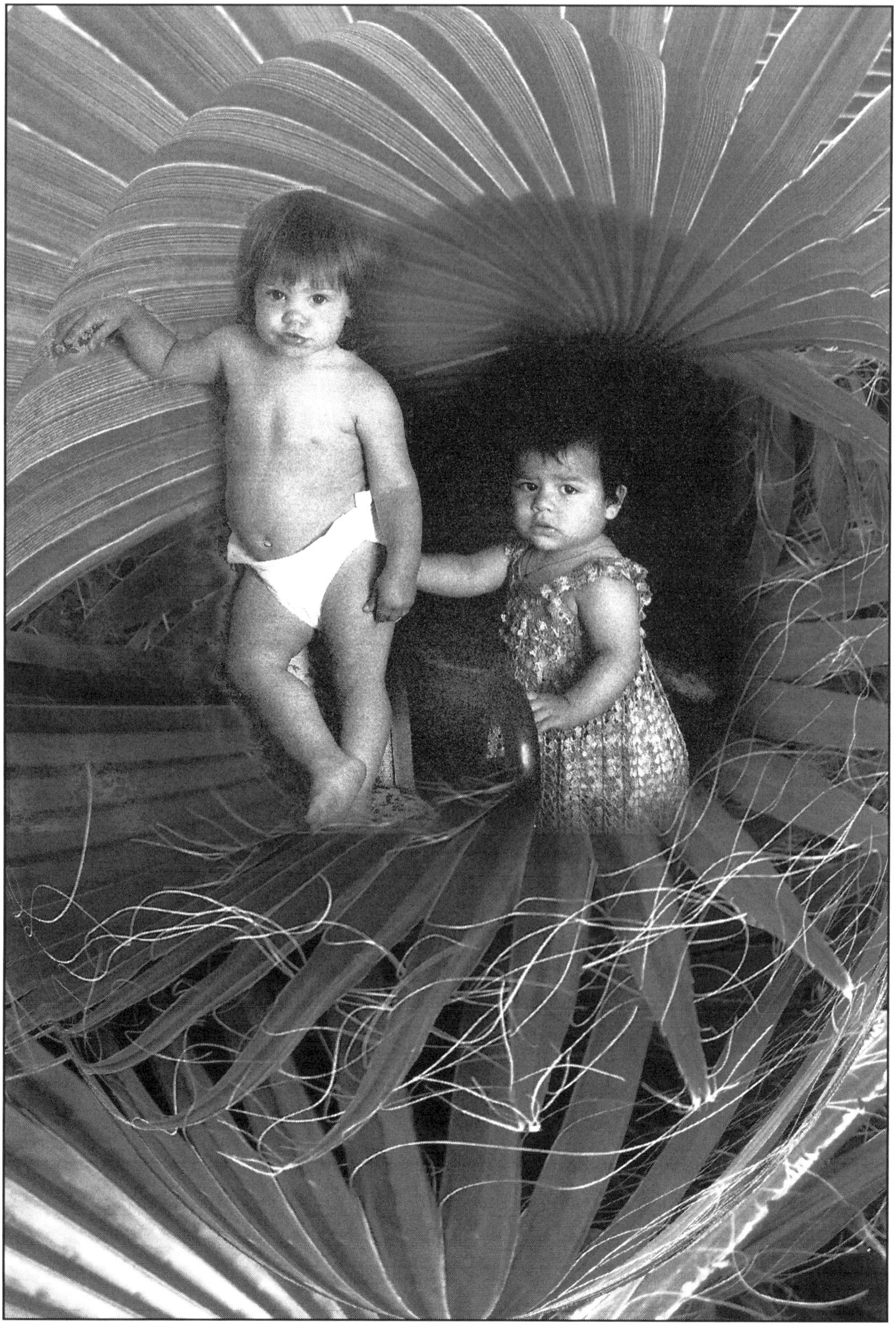

CHAPTER II

Childwork

Nothing is left absolute by modern physics but equations—and these are thoughts. Obviously this unexpected outcome of mechanical materialism is not due to the fact that it was materialistic, but to the fact that it was not materialistic enough. By giving thoughts and sensuous qualities a purely subjective and fictitious existence, excluded from the reality of matter, the mechanical materialists at once established a field of non-material reality which contradicted the basis of their procedure. (Christopher Caudwell, 7)

·~·

It's important to look at childwork, because children are not cattle to be "cared for." It is not the case that one person can "care for" twenty children as well as two people can. Nor can two people "care for" twenty children as well as four people can.

Childwork is labor intensive.

It is true that you can regiment twenty children to such a degree that two people can "care for" them, but you gets what you labors for. If you treat them like cattle, being humans, they become a pretty deranged kind of cattle. Childwork is labor intensive and it is intense labor, the most intense in human experience. Also, not just anyone can do it well. Childwork is skilled labor. Nor is it the case that childworkers are infinitely variable, so that one can replace another like workers on an assembly line.

Children are not auto bodies.

It is important to look at childwork because it is subject to a complex set of laws of its own, ones at least as complex as economic laws and far less amenable to manipulation. These "laws," these interrelations, are largely invisible.

Tillie Olsen recorded some glimpses of this in her book *Silences*, documenting the crushing weight of patriarchy over the efforts of women to write. Here she quotes Sally Bingham:

> My grandmother, who wrote and sold short stories at one point in her life, before raising six children, used to claim with some bitterness that bearing and raising children drained a woman's creativity. Her disappointment reminds me of my own failure to solve the problems of raising children and carrying on a fulltime career. I haven't lost my sap, but I have certainly lost time; five out of the past ten years, at least, have been "lost" to bearing and raising three boys, and the end is not yet in sight. My work is reduced to five or six hours a week, always subject to interruptions and cancellations; and yet I do not regret the shape my life has taken, although it is not the one I would have chosen, ten years ago…
>
> I don't believe there is a solution…which recognizes the emotional complexities involved. A life without children is, I feel, an impoverished life for most women; yet life with children imposes demands that consume energy and imagination as well as time, and that cannot all be delegated—even supposing there were a delegate available….
>
> A woman's response to a child's illness is part of her whole involvement with that child; it is not logical, perhaps, and yet it may be essential to that child's belief that his mother cares for him. I cannot imagine continuing to work when one of my children is running a high fever or is in pain; my mind would be totally distracted. Nor can I easily imagine leaving him in someone else's care; my thoughts would still be preempted. (233-234)

"The emotional complexities involved…"

"the child's belief that his mother cares for him…"

"my thoughts would still be preempted…"

(my consciousness still occupied)

This means:

"I would still be childworking."

It's important to look at the nature of childwork because it is the work which people do on a daily basis that defines their lives.

Every day

is where the hours of your life

are located

Your life (time)

Your self .

It's important to look at the nature of childwork because, more than anything else, it has defined the lives of women. Not only outside of women (what expectations and beliefs about women have been formed), but inside of women as well, because it is real work. The majority of men, who have never done it, don't understand this. Men see it as the passive "accompaniment" of women and children. This vision that men have of women and children together is simply that: what they see: women and children together. They define this relationship as a state of being, not work. They think that all women have to do is

"be"

with children.

The labor involved has never been recognized. Even today, women with children are asked if they work.

"Do you work?"

And many women, whose hearts shrink at the question, have been conditioned to say, "No. I stay at home with my child(ren)." Because the process of giving birth (those few hours) is unconscious (animal) work, the entire process of reproduction (tending to all of the animal needs and emotional needs of children; preventing them from killing themselves; reproducing the entire social system in them), is seen as animal work, not even dignified with the description "work."

Women (are) mothers.

Men (do) work.

Women are.
Men do.

This definition of women and men

is at the core of patriarchal ideology.

"The reluctance to call caring and care giving work is perhaps one of the most critical factors in reinforcing the notion that care giving is a private rather than public or collective social responsibility" (Nancy Folbre, 12).

The notion that women are and men do,

the notion that childwork is not real labor,

is as fantastic as the notion that the world is flat.

·⁘·

Work is not just something we do and get it over with and there, outside ourselves, is the result.

Work is energy.

Energy is not a two-dimensional force which just starts somewhere and goes somewhere else, point A to point B.

Energy is a creative process.

Human beings are a form of (partly) conscious energy, and the work they do is a conscious (human) directing of energy. (If it is unconscious, it isn't "work": it's energy working on its own terms, throbbing stars and throbbing the human heart without any thoughtful effort on our part at all).

Energy has laws which we don't understand, but can observe. One of them is that it transforms itself ceaselessly. It just keeps truckin' along through one form into another, alive (to our eyes) or otherwise.

It does this in sidereal time, geological time, recorded time and unrecorded time; it does it in boogie time, in two-four time, on the bosses time, in your free time, at the proper time, at the wrong time,

in no time at all.

When we die, for example, the energy in our bodies goes into bacteria which decompose into the soil, where it is sucked up by plants into nourishment for plant energy…. Or in cremation, much of our body matter (which is only one form of energy) is transformed into heat energy which soars up and joins the energy in the atmosphere…

As far as energy is concerned, nothing is ever wasted and nothing is ever lost and nothing ever stays in the same form

forever.

One of the observable facts about energy is that it changes whatever it travels through (and what it travels through is another form of itself).

Human work is one of many forms of energy. It doesn't just transform whatever it is humans are working on, it transforms the humans themselves.

Bass players get calloused fingers from their work. Fishers and peasants whose work exposes them constantly to the sun and wind, develop leathery skin.

Women who dive for pearls develop muscular bodies and great lung power.

People are transformed by their work in far less visible ways.

Those who hunt develop a keen sense of hearing. Playwrights develop a keen sense of human conflict. Writers organize thought into word sequences and become articulate. Whatever human or animal faculties are exercised in daily work, transform the workers and not only "the worked upon." That's the nature of energy.

The daily exercise of childwork develops certain characteristics in the workers who perform it every day just as certainly as daily diving produces strong lungs. Because human organization assigns childwork to women, those characteristics have come to be identified with women, and indeed they form a great part of what most women are and have always been, not because women were born with such characteristics, but because the work they do produces the need to develop such qualities.

(An Aside on Ignorance)

In the past, serious analysis of childwork was not undertaken, first because it was not recognized as "work," but perceived as an inevitable part of nature. Second, because those who traditionally did studies (men) remotely approaching childwork have been much more interested in their own formation (how it affected them) than in how it formed their mothers. Their mothers were never seen to be "formed" by childwork anyway, but were assumed to be born with all of the qualities such work produced in them.

Today serious studies of women, their lives, and their work are finally being done, but primary research on the nature of childwork still needs to be done. One reason it's been neglected is that women tend to be biased in the same way men are in the sense that they are more interested in how childwork formed them as children and what role it played in the internalizing of their oppression. Another is that some of our best thinkers and theorists (and this is no accident) have been women who have not had children.

Also, there is a dangerous anti-child bias in some feminist writing—a devaluation of "women's work." Since childwork seems to preclude any other significant creative activity or independence in life under the existing division of labor, children are sometimes dimly (sadly, patriarchally) perceived as "enemy." This is not representative of feminist thought, as many feminists celebrate their children, but rather a dangerous undercurrent more a product of neglect to develop certain themes than a conscious statement. Women have reason to fear what children represent for them in this patriarchal system.

The sheer overwhelming weight of women's oppression described in the (now scientific) studies conducted by women obscure the (primary) (related) development of women by the nature of "their" work itself. The urgency to change the existing power relations drains energy and thought-power into diverse forms of struggle and resistance. But to develop a powerful theory of gender relations, such work needs to include a scientific analysis of that which most women all over the world all have had in common and continue to have in common, childwork. Not only childwork as it forms women's social relations (some stabs have been made at that), but

childwork as it forms women

by its very nature as work

apart from all the human circumstance surrounding it.

I don't mean to underestimate the power of the social relations surrounding childwork, only to abstract out of that entanglement the truth about the nature of the work itself, the qualities it demands and develops in whoever does it or would do it, women or men in any social system, past, present, or future.

The most important characteristic of childwork, the one which has the most far-reaching effects on those who perform it, is that it is completely absorbing for years. In the first years, it absorbs workers, not eight hours a day, not sixteen hours a day, but twenty-four hours a day. Unlike other kinds of work, it is inescapable. There is no shift which can ever be left empty, no time when nobody can be attending to it. Even when asleep, childworkers must be "on duty" to be awakened at any moment to work (expend conscious human effort), and frequently are.

Now, when a worker sets out to carve a tree trunk

into a boat,

no matter how absorbing the work might be,

no matter how important it is to the survival of the worker

to get that boat built,

the worker can set down the boat carving tool,

and rest a minute.

Eat, maybe.

While the worker is eating (or the hunter is taking a piss),

the work at hand

may be released.

The mind may be released.

And workers and hunters look forward to eating and pissing,

not only because it feels so good

but because it gives them

predictable moments of unstructured time

(and time is what it's all about).

The boat maker and the hunter

just might give themselves

a little minute or two

now and then

to daydream (rest their consciousness)

or maybe to consciously

ponder for a minute something they noticed

about the form of the boat

or the habits of animals

which might lead nowhere

but might just lead to a better boat or a faster kill.

During those moments,

not much is lost.

The boat might be slightly delayed,

but it's worth the risk if the boat may be improved.

The hunter might lose sight of the prey

but there are always other prey,

and in any case,

no hunter would do such dreaming in hot pursuit, and

hot pursuit is a very small proportion of hunting work.

During the first years, for childworkers, the risk of momentarily resting consciousness, or diverting it from the work at hand, even for the duration of a piss, is not the risk of a little delay in the outcome of the work.

In the early stages, a childworker who disengages consciousness from childwork for one minute, for one second of one minute, risks human death. The death of a close friend and relative. The death of all previously invested, (life)time in the child (as such, self death). The death of any future benefits that could be derived from that child (co-operative labor; emotional rewards). Emotional pain.

The emotional rewards of childwork are not quantifiable by linear methods but are quite real, as anyone who has ever been warmed by the smile of a child or been disintegrated into laughter by them knows.

This too can be brutally eliminated by one minute of relaxed consciousness. The avoidance of such loss and pain in itself is a significant incentive to perform childwork diligently.

·⁂·

Childwork is of a very different nature than the work of the hunter or the boatmaker, both qualitatively and quantitatively different in reference to time. Childwork may (depending partly on the number of children involved), afford a few unstructured moments during its performance, but they are far fewer than those afforded by other kinds of work, in both frequency and duration, and are less predictable.

When thinking cannot be planned,

thinking molds itself to its opportunities.

Childwork itself doesn't preclude human thought, but influences its mode. I think that from this arises fabled "women's intuition." It is nonlinear because extended linear thought is precluded by childwork to a great degree. It is thought which has been described by poets and mystics and people who have studied non-western cultures, as global thought. In and of itself it does not produce either enlightenment or better life(times) for women and men any more than linear thought does. It is simply a different mode, making more accessible different insights.

Not having the leisure to examine perceived stimuli one by one, separate from each other, or separate from the senses, or separate from the emotions, this kind of peculiarly intense thought apprehends, calibrates, and judges many stimuli simultaneously, in relation to (not abstracted from) each other. It can be achieved by the conscious release of directed thought (meditation) as well as forcibly conditioned by childwork.

Such non-linear thinking is reinforced considerably by interacting constantly with children, especially those who have not reached the age of reason, which is to say, for six or seven years. Before then, children can't or won't relinquish their own perceptions in favor of the perceptions of adults, except by brute force or by interaction on the children's own terms.

Childworkers are forcibly and frequently drawn into the global parameters of children's thought, not merely out of a sense of wonder, but by the objective and constant necessity to control the children.

To perceive reality freshly, with the eyes of a child, to any degree, is a valuable skill, and one which childwork develops in its workers to some degree under all conditions, as a byproduct of these forced marches into the childworker's own "intuition" as well as into the uncharted universe of children's thought.

·⸻·

When a non-childworker (with no previous experience of primary childwork) observes a childworker in the course of some simple task, the observer might note the childworker bend over and retrieve something (a twig; a peanut; a rock) from the hands of a crawling infant. This is done "automatically" with no fanfare, perhaps without breaking stride or breaking the sequence of social interaction between the observer and the childworker. It's possible that this slight gesture would go unperceived altogether, unremarked in the mind of an inexperienced observer.

What the childworker has experienced may not be visible, but is of momentous consequence to the child and to the consciousness of the childworker. Early childwork especially is a life and death situation in which a failure of intelligence or a slight lapse of attention can lead to death. There are very few jobs which have been assigned to men in the human way of organizing work, which are comparable. The closest most men ever come to such conditioning is in war, and then, only in daily combat. And at that, their experience is measured more often in days or months, and rarely in years.

Men, inexperienced with such critical conditioning, make a great to-do over it. They recognize among themselves that outwitting death on a daily basis produces great stamina, resourcefulness, kinesthetic wit, and a kind of bare bones pragmatism much admired

in themselves.

Ask a childworker how many ways children can find to kill themselves, how many ways the world around them can kill them independent of their efforts, how many ways the interaction of both variables can produce injury and death, and you will find that the ways that men have invented to kill each other are quite limited by comparison.

Childwork demands and develops in its workers a degree of *self discipline* only faintly echoed by the results of the brutal and ritualistic military training men have contrived to impose such self-discipline on each other in the interests of surviving and/or fulfilling their own murderous intentions toward each other. It's work that commonly produces a degree of self discipline, concomitant with a sense of responsibility, far greater, far more intense, and far more concrete than any other form of human labor.

In the present humanly organized division of labor, childwork is assigned to women, and much of what passes for "passivity" in many women is a form of stoicism conditioned by their work.

·~·

Commonly, childwork demands and develops in its workers a degree of self-control over the human impulses of anger and aggression so unknown to the working experience of men that the free (open!) expression of both has become identified as "male" by definition.

Endowed with human minds, children can conceive of performing complex human activities long before they are either physically capable of them or aware of their (often injurious) consequences. It's the nature of children, however, to attempt every kind of human activity as soon as it can be conceived of, possible or not, safe or not. As a result, childworkers are daily in the position of frustrating the deeply felt desires of children.

This produces deeply felt rage against the childworkers.

Moreover, childworkers are forced to witness all of the searing humiliation subsequent to these many attempts at full-fledged competence. The pain of these profoundly humiliating experiences—falling down, being refused a desired object, messing in the pants, closing the door on the fingers, misunderstood messages in very clear (to the child) language:

infinitely repeated defeats pounding her/his helplessness into the striving consciousness of the child.

This pain, as well as the often physical pain of the experiences themselves, produce deeply felt rage, which is targeted at the childworker.

The childworker is to the child not only the source of great pleasure, support, solace and love, but a boss. Children experience feelings toward their "bosses" in common with adult feelings toward bosses, no matter how benevolent the "boss," but even more intense. The relation between a helpless child and the childworker who is perceived by the child to be the major source of joy, pain, opportunity, frustration, food, encouragement, misunderstanding, defeat,

of life itself

is also the most singular despotism of human experience.

This is our first power relationship, and no matter how benevolent that power may be, it constitutes a position of dominance over another human. It is struggled against and resented with all of the physical, intellectual, and emotional resources at the disposal of the dominated human. Children aren't rational. They perceive the almighty figure of their primary childworker(s) as the direct cause of their pain, defeats, humiliations, frustrations. Not being "cattle" that the childworker is "caring for," children strike back.

   The deep ambivalence of feeling experienced toward the primary childworker (who is both the source of all good and the perceived "enemy" of the child's emerging self) has far reaching consequences for human development which are central to the institution of patriarchy as it is internally constructed in all of us. My insight into this reality came through the work of Dorothy Dinnerstein, who examined this relationship with great acuity. I want to discuss her observations a little further on,

but what I wish to point out here, in its external social construct,

is the way in which childwork conditions its workers to suppress anger and aggression, because childworkers are human. They are not the almighty gods very young children perceive them to be. When children lash out against their own painful helplessness; when they rage at their childworkers, they do indeed hurt them. A childworker who is spit on by a two year old for being taken in out of the rain; who is slapped, kicked, screamed at in primordial fury in the course of performing the needed services to keep a child safe and sound; who has laboriously prepared meals thrown in her face; toys lovingly accumulated, made, or bought smashed in fury; who is subjected to nerve grating hours of sustained whining and irritability for events outside of her control (teething; loss of a person or object),

must

forcibly,

develop an iron self-control.

For knowing that a child is helpless and ignorant doesn't reduce the immediate human reaction to being screamed at, does not lessen the tension of hours of implacable whining; does not reduce the wild fury that wild fury sparks. That knowledge only imposes the necessity to control the self. It doesn't change the human self or the human impulse to return blow for blow, hurt for hurt.

No childworker is ever entirely successful at suppressing such human reactions, but all childworkers are forced, daily, into rational behavior against the upswellings of anger, frustration, and even fury that are periodically inherent to childwork under any conditions and an enormous component of childwork under prevailing conditions. In the present humanly organized division of labor, childwork is assigned to women. And much of what passes for "meekness" in women is self-control conditioned by such work. The immense psychological demands of such self-control require exhausting, sustained, invisible, sometimes soul-wrenching

effort.

Out of the cumulative efforts at self-control over years of intimate, grueling struggle with the irrational forces embodied in children and embodied in the childworkers themselves, is born much of the quiet, patient strength commonly associated with women—an inner strength and power conspicuously lacking in the untempered, unconditioned, impatient (unexamined and therefore destructive) aggression of so many men. Men are largely isolated from this self-transcending process which has no other parallel in human life.

·⇜⇝·

    A worker who works on boats all day long

    will become attuned to the beauty and utility of boats; will come to appreciate boats for their own sake.

    A non boat builder can get on the boat and ride it across a body of water without thinking about its design or its production;

    might, in fact, be quite bored by the conversation of the boatmaker, all full of boat information and boat wonder.

    A builder of boats, or a sailor of boats, or any person whose daily work includes intimate interaction with boats,

    respects boats.

    A slave, who is forced to split rocks, who hates the work, who hates the brutal conditions of the work,

    learns a lot about and respects

    rocks.

    And it needs to be said,

    because it is the truth:

    Almost always

childworkers are more likely to respect children

respect human life outside of their own human life

respect the future of human life (which children are)

than non-childworkers.

Sensitive non-childworkers may develop a great respect for human life outside of childwork, but the probabilities of its development are more random, and it is always more abstract.

◆⋙◈⋘◆

There are conditions outside of childwork which make it so unbearable that childworkers can be induced to actually abuse children, but these conditions are not produced by childwork itself. They are variables which act on a constant and that constant is a respect for human life which is promoted by childwork under all conditions.

Given the vulnerability of infants and children, their survival over the ages under all conditions, no matter how brutal, either for themselves or the childworkers, is incontrovertible proof that such respect is en(gender)ed in childworkers by childwork. There is no "childworker instinct" any more than there is a "rock-splitter instinct" or a "boat-building instinct." In fact childworkers at any given moment during the work, are quite pleased indeed if someone comes along and offers to relieve them of the job, even for a few minutes, just as all workers are.

The compelling nature of childwork does not reside in the bodies of childworkers, but is located in children, in the objective requirements of performing childwork successfully, no matter who does it.

◆⋙◈⋘◆

(An Aside on the Ownership of Instinct)

An instinct is a very strong behavior pattern. It's something on the order of pulling your arms up to protect your eyes and your head when you are about to receive a blow. It is automatic, powerful, unvarying unconscious behavior which always has as its biological objective the defense or preservation of an individual's life. Not some other individual, but the life of the possessor of the instinct.

Babies have an instinct to suck (on anything). This behavior on the part of babies is integral to their survival. Women don't have an instinct to give milk to babies. Their survival is not in any way connected to giving milk to babies. Babies suck very well. Women who have never breastfed before or who have never observed other women breastfeeding are notoriously incompetent at it when they first do it, and often cause much frustration to babies. The desire to breastfeed a baby comes from the physical pleasure it involves and comes in great measure from wanting the baby to thrive. This desire is no more remarkable in an individual woman than the automatic reaction of a policeman, who finds a baby somewhere, to get it someplace where it can get fed. This is a human desire, not an instinct exclusive to women.

In fact, men who do nurture children develop elevated levels of oxytocin.

> The medical "opposite" of testosterone is oxytocin, the so-called nurturance hormone. It reaches very high levels in nursing mothers, but also increases significantly in the bloodstream of fathers who spend time in close proximity to their newborn children. It makes a person feel loving and caring. (Nancy Folbre, 11)

What is exclusive to women is a desire to breastfeed predicated on the discomfort of swollen breasts. As an unconscious instinct, separate from the conscious ideas about breastfeeding that an individual woman might have, it has no strength at all. In contexts in which women are taught that their animal functions are disgusting, women are revolted by the idea of breastfeeding and simply don't do it if any other way can be found to feed the baby. Upper class women in many historical periods have quite happily given over that (optional) part of childwork to other childworkers, "wet nurses," whose breasts are not full because they have an instinct to feed the child, but because the child (quite outside of them) is used to stimulate milk production by sucking,

and because the nurses get paid to do it.

If they weren't paid to do it, they wouldn't seek out such work. They would just let their breasts dry and work at something else.

Many women, regardless of class, don't do it because they believe it will change the shape of their breasts. In my own mother's generation, in U.S. middle class white culture, women were discouraged (by men, the defenders of the myth of maternal instinct) from breastfeeding on the grounds that children needed to be fed on a precise clockwork schedule. If breastfeeding were an instinct, a powerful survival mechanism beyond the control of human consciousness, you would have seen women furtively, desperately hiding in closets or under the covers with their babies, gasping to do their bodies' bidding, compulsively thrusting their breasts at babies just as they would throw their hands in front of their faces as something flew at their faces.

Such was not the case.

Some women questioned the wisdom of the patriarchal authority figures (male doctors) who advised women not to breastfeed, and many more women chafed at the rigid, arbitrary feeding schedules, but by and large, women accepted it. Babies accepted the bottles given to them in place of the breast, quite nicely. In fact babies uniformly prefer bottles to the breast and once on the bottle, refuse to return to the breast, which in itself is a statement about the strength of "nature's arrangement."

The instinct being violated by this arrangement wasn't female instinct but the babies' instinct to have their hunger satisfied when they were hungry. And babies did scream, did writhe under their covers, did protest, not for lack of breasts, but for lack of food, for hours at a time, on those rigid feeding schedules.

Indeed, mammals produce milk after birth. Mammal babies suck it out, which feels very good. Eventually, mammal babies develop teeth and it no longer feels good at all and mammal babies are forced to find their food elsewhere.

There is no instinct involved in childwork.

I keep repeating this because the strength of the myth obscures a very important truth which I am also going to repeat, and that is that the compelling nature of childwork does not reside in the bodies of childworkers: it's located in children. Women don't have an instinct to feed and take care of them any more than men have an instinct to neglect or murder them. The fact that, by and large, it is women who feed them when they're fed and men who murder them when they get murdered, isn't due to the instincts of either party.

Feeding and nurturing behavior on the part of women is largely a product of their social conditioning by children, directly through the children or through other women who have had long experience childworking: their mothers.

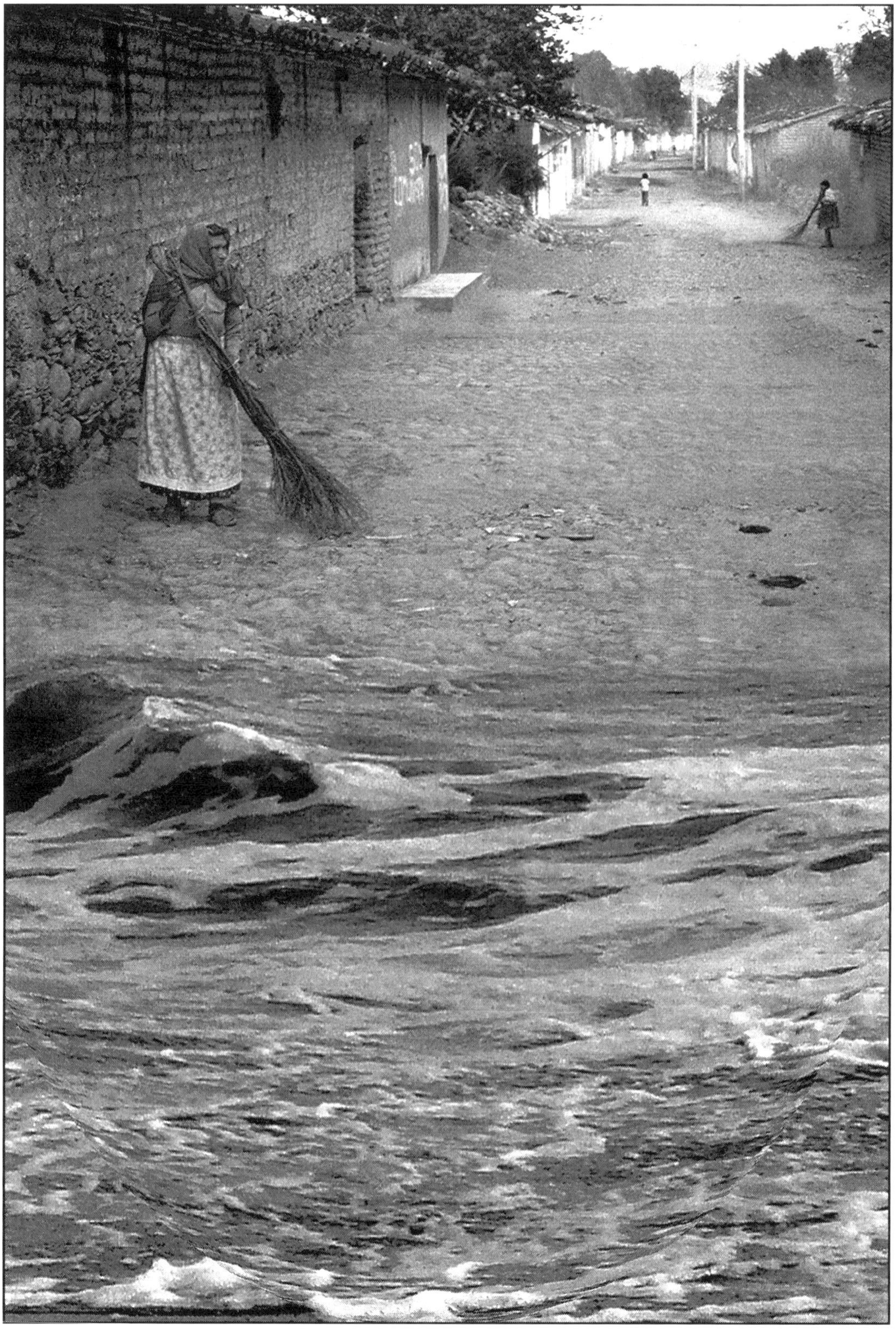

CHAPTER III

The Politics of Progress

Men are not fully socialized into humanity, because in patriarchy most men have spent their working life(times) divorced (to a great degree) from the socializing influence of the majority of humanity (women and children): divorced from the social relations of reproduction.

The social relations of reproduction (by themselves) are inherently beneficial to human life. The objective interests of children consistently dovetail with the interests of all humanity.

The same cannot be said of the social relations of production separate from the social relations of reproduction.

❦

There are many progressive movements across the world. By progressive movements, I mean attempts by humans to take power over their lives in ways that will improve the conditions of life for most people. These include the struggles of women to take power over their bodies; the struggles of farmers to harvest their seed for replanting rather than having to pay protection money to the big agrichemical companies; the movement to conserve energy and develop renewable sources of energy; to protect the environment; to give workers power over their working conditions; to recognize the love of men for men and women for women. You live in a country which spends a lot of resources unsuccessfully trying to stamp out these movements (and many others like them), here and all over the world.

Such movements represent in humans an ever more conscious use of energy, to survive better. (More humanly. Less like non-human machines or other animals, wild or domestic). For a good part of the last century, many millions of people the world over hoped that a new and better order which would improve the conditions of life for most people would come in the form of a political/social revolution. Their hopes were informed by brilliant analyses of two social philosophers, Karl Marx (1818-1883) and

Frederick Engels (1820-1895).

They were men with a stunning insight. They saw that the social organization of humans (and therefore who was poor and miserable and who was rich and had power over their own lives and others' lives), was directly related to how societies produced their food and wealth. And they traced, very accurately, a pattern of human social organization which produced

classes of people

whose poorness or richness (whose power over their own lives and others' lives) was, in economic terms at least, directly proportional to their distance from the ownership of the means to produce such food and wealth.

Stay with me here: I want to show how the great hopes and struggles for socialism, which was supposed to provide the better world so many worked for, have not been fulfilled. One of the reasons was that class analysis (the analysis of the social relations of production) alone is an incomplete way of looking at human societies. There was no concordant analysis of the social relations of reproduction (which were not so transparent to the men seeking revolution).

According to the Marxists, in the earliest hunting and gathering societies there were comparatively small class divisions, and they described the organization of such societies as "primitive communism." With the development of domesticated animals and agriculture, they noted the development of the social institution of slavery, followed by feudalism and, with the advent of machines, capitalism. All of these forms of human social organization (and their many transitional mixtures and varieties) flowed out of changes in the means of production: sets of relationships determined by the ownership of the means of production. (Feudal lords owned the land; later, capitalists owned the machinery).

These ideas were conditioned by the nineteenth-century view of evolution and the nineteenth-century assumption that progress was inevitable. Given the course of human history since the nineteenth century, and given our present day understanding of our biological history, the assumption that humans move on to ever greater improvements, or that real human progress is an inexorable path forward seems naive indeed. But that doesn't make their insight concerning economic classes any less valuable. Class is a powerful determiner of social identity, social structure, and political movement.

Marx and Engels set out to analyze these forms of organization in a materialist fashion, that is, not as ordained by some god, but seeking, as Engels wrote,

...the ultimate cause and the great moving power of all important historic events in the economic development of society, in the changes in the modes of production and exchange, in the consequent division of society into distinct classes, and in the struggles of these classes against one another. (*Socialism: Utopian and Scientific*)

Which is to say, impelled by human self-interest.

The analytical tool they developed to help us consciously understand (and therefore change) human social organization—class analysis—so well describes things that are true—is so powerful, that even today, all over the world there are social and political struggles consciously informed by its insights.

The two philosophers set out to understand (so that it could be eliminated) what they justly described as "man's inhumanity to man," and their work provided insights essential to ending man's inhumanity to man as well as man's inhumanity to women and children incidental to man's inhumanity to man,

which is enormous.

But their analysis of man's specific inhumanity to women

never fully got off the ground;

and they didn't analyze man's specific inhumanity to children (aside from how it is incidental to man's inhumanity to man), at all.

This isn't suprising and we shouldn't fault them for it, but it is urgent that women analyze the inhumanity of man to women and children which is not incidental to man's inhumanity to man, because it will be the understanding or failure to understand human social organization

by those women and men who are giving birth to the future

which will determine what kind of a world, if any, there will be for children and women and men to live in.

Marx and Engels were aware that women were especially oppressed. Engels, rummaging around some very early thoughts that led to later work, quotes himself and Marx as saying "The first division of labor is that between man and woman for the propagation of children." He also wrote that "the first class oppression coincides with that of the female sex by the male" (*Origins of the Family*). He associated this with the appearance of monogamous marriage, when actually it predated it, but basically his observation was correct. Two different social groups got created *by the different nature of the work they did* (not marriage) and the relations between the two groups came to be that of a dominant group and a subordinate group.

Men came to be exclusively involved in work which men call productive labor (producing material goods), while women produced (in addition to material goods) socialized humans (including men) and time (for men). It's interesting that not even the most enlightened men ever considered or named this kind of work "productive" and an entire analysis of their self-esteem could be based on that phenomenon. Suffice it to say here that both kinds of work are productive, but that they produce different social relations (in and of themselves).

The great body of the work of Marx and Engels was taken up with an analysis of the social relations of production as men understand it. They didn't spend so much time analyzing the social relations of the work specific to women, which they called "reproduction." Their vision of children was static (compare the word "reproduction" to the word "production."). "Reproduction" sees children as something pulled out of women, each one much like the next, one Kleenex after another in the bottomless female Kleenex box feeding into the social relations of production: the capitalist wanted personal ones to inherit his wealth and an army of others to labor in his interest; the workers wanted them so that they would bring in more wealth to the houses of the workers, or at least bring in more wealth in the old age of the workers.

Why women ever wanted them is unaccounted for in this analysis for no amount of (remote) economic rewards for having them could be equal to the labor which children extracted from women (even when there were any economic rewards promised, which was not always the case for men and is certainly not the case today, for women or men workers).

Why people want children simply does not lend itself to this kind of economic analysis. I believe that this is subject to empirical proof: that if the total income produced by children which is in any way transferred to their parents is measured against the accumulated income that could be produced by a man and a woman working solely for themselves throughout their life(times), their net worth at the end of their lives would far outweigh whatever they produce or accumulate for themselves by having children.

So, in the Marxist analysis, the fact that women had them must be due to a state of ignorance as to their origins, uncontrollable sexual urges, absolute slavery in relation to men, or

instinct!

Yes, indeedy.

Today, in societies where contraception is available to women, and where absolute slavery to men is not the case, millions of women go right on having children (though not so many as women do in countries without contraception available to them), often in complicity with men, and in absolute defiance of their economic interests.

In the Marxist conception of the social relations of reproduction, men, even workers, only see children as a source of profit to themselves. Workers are not that dumb, as any woman who has been unintentionally impregnated by one and had to announce it to the worker

can tell you.

Even in the case of the most male chauvinist pig workers in history, this has simply never been the whole truth. In fact, many male workers (inconsistently) make great sacrifices which are not in their immediate or remote self-interest on behalf of their children (male children, most especially). And childworkers make far greater sacrifices (consistently), (for both male and female children).

Just who is the boss here?

Could it be that those cutesy little babies have power over us all?

·~·

The Marxist answer to the oppression of women was formulated by Lenin, who led a revolution using Marxist insights. It's an answer which has never been substantially modified by many progressive thinkers, which is, (and I quote Lenin): "...to draw the women into socially productive labor, extricate them from 'domestic slavery,' free them of their stultifying and humiliating resignation to the perpetual and exclusive atmosphere of the kitchen and nursery" (*On International Women's Day*).

·~·

Leaving the kitchen aside for a moment, let's look into the nursery.

Who is excluding whom?

Are we to conclude: men are free, happy, and liberated because they have excluded children from their working lives,

and so women will be free, happy, and liberated only when they, too, have excluded children from their working lives?

Are children to become a special social group (class) whose most productive and creative hours are to be spent with another special class of people, "professional child-workers" in some sanitized ghetto apart from the rest of human society?

·⁌⁍·

In the different versions of "socialism" found in countries today where animal want has been lessened (as in China) or almost eliminated (as in Denmark) and where, as a result, purely human urges can now be attended to by everyone to some degree, patriarchy still exists. It's been dealt some heavy blows because all women no longer need to be absolutely dependent on men economically. Women have been introduced more fully into the social relations of production. That was what socialist forms of government have promised and those promises have been fulfilled to a meaningful degree. Much of formal patriarchy (patriarchal laws) have been eliminated, but patriarchy still exists.

Progressives everywhere would like to believe that patriarchy is just some kind of hangover that will go away. But it won't ever go away just by changing the social relations of production. It never has been changed essentially in any system of what men consider "production" since surpluses came into being.

Only a radical change in the social relations of reproduction will eliminate patriarchy.

Men must be integrated into the social relations of reproduction. Not as paternalistic "benefactors" or "helpers"; not as paternalistic "supervisors" or liberal paternalistic "approvers looking on"; not as Sunday head-patters, not as paters (as we know them), not as patriarchs, but as

workers.

Men, not only women, must be reared by children.

The whole economy needs to be rebalanced. As Nancy Folbre writes:

> ...caregivers in general and mothers in particular subsidize the market economy. And there is a sense in which the market economy is sucking them dry, just as it is sucking up other natural resources like clean air, sea turtles, tropical hardwoods and a stable climate. It's time for the market economy to get weaned, grasp the meaning of "no," learn to use the potty and offer some pay-back. (11)

·⁌⁍·

Children must be drawn into socially productive labor, socializing adults and sharing some measure of meaningful production and maintenance tasks. Children aren't as useless and stupid as we try to educate them to be. They're as seriously underestimated, underutilized and underappreciated as women ever have been. Children need to be freed of their stultifying and humiliating assignation (for it has never been resignation) to the perpetual and exclusive atmosphere of the kitchen and nursery.

What is the role (social relation) of a father toward his child in a socialist state (in any of their present forms) which is essentially different from the role of a father who has successfully provided economic sustenance for his child in a capitalist state? What force is built into any state (up to now) that will ever change the relative triviality of that role?

After the material goods have been provided, what organic relationship is left? How meaningful is it to bounce this stranger, about whom you know relatively little, on your knee on weekend afternoons? If you aren't or never have been a childworker, you're not likely to truly comprehend (and therefore be engaged or deeply interested in or even appreciate) who is in front of you, much less be profoundly transformed by who is in front of you.

I recognize that there are individual differences among men in the depth and scope (or lack thereof) in the relations they have with their children—and that men's conscious intentions toward their children in most cases favor what men consider to be the children's wellbeing. "Providing" is the one social relation men have always esteemed themselves for in relation to their families. It is also the one role which they have ever performed with a great degree of consistency which was important to women and children. Outside of this role, they may have only sentimental importance to their families.

Sentimental importance is like romantic love.

Pretty ephemeral at best.

It is true that there are individual men who have raised children by themselves, genuinely childworking, who learn to cherish their children and bond with them in ways we usually consider "maternal." There are also men who are aware that they are missing out on some valuable, even precious child relations because they are forced into the brutalizing conditions of "men's work" in the prevailing social relations of production—men who even envy the time childworkers enjoy with children. There is a spectrum of male behavior and male attitudes toward children with extremes at both ends, but the generalization that women are the primary childworkers holds in the vast majority of cases, and those primary relationships are qualitatively different in scope and depth than any other relationships in human life.

⁕

Men have never been fully socialized and much can be said about the benefits of their socialization by children.

So far we've looked at the introduction of an alternative (global) mode of thought, which widens perception, conditioned by childwork, and the deep (sustained) self-discipline such work demands. It also develops a deep (concrete) self-control in relation to "other than self."

All of these qualities are indispensable to an improved social order.

Childwork conditions its workers in many ways, but perhaps (as a promise of happiness, of emotional fulfillment) the most important is the conditioning it provides to even *recognize* many real human needs, and subsequently the development of the skills to fulfill them.

One of the problems with the economic "materialist" analysis Marxists adhered to in the past is its emphasis on visible need. More than a century later we have a much better grasp of the nature of "matter" in "(mater)ialism," (energy), and need to extend the materialist analysis accordingly.

A painful fact about the great majority of the privileged gender group of men which is experienced almost universally by the underclass which services them is that they are so often emotional parasites. Some of the deepest pain and most mutilating suffering inherent to patriarchy are the deep wounds of these leachings because it is our human selves bled by this, not only our animal selves.

Like the humiliation of rape, which is most often expressed in the emotional (and sometimes physical) mutilation of a subclass by a dominant one, (Feminists know that "rape is sexualized aggression, not aggressive sexuality"), this is an element of patriarchy incomprehensible to most men, as they have never experienced it, qualitatively or quantitatively, as women have. Women have always serviced them emotionally, under all conditions of oppression or privilege, and such services are rarely returned in kind, quality, or sustained frequency.

This parasitism is infantile.

Childworkers, who are in direct contact with infants, often recognize this about men. ("They're just big babies! God, they're like 2-year olds! They act like children!")

>Echoes
>> echoes
>>> echoes
>>>> down the centuries.

Indeed, men often do not advance into emotional maturity for several reasons unavoidable in the patriarchal division of labor.

One of the major reasons is that it is childwork itself which demands a reversal of social relations from child to childworker.

The indifference of men to the emotional needs of women does not arise only out of gender class contempt (the inability to even perceive women as fully human) as even those few men who consciously recognize, or try to recognize women as human, often fail to nurture as they are nurtured.

The failure is due, in great measure, to their inability to even *recognize* the form and depth of such needs. It is like someone who has never had any relationship to airplanes other than being a passenger in them trying to maintain and repair them. Unlike the machinery of airplanes, however, the machinery of human emotional being isn't always so visible (until it breaks down altogether, which may be the only time men ever notice it), nor accessible to purely intellectual intelligence. An intelligence of *feeling* is required, another mode of thought, perception, apprehension,

an intelligence never concretely required by the kind of work most men spend their life(times) doing and which is therefore undeveloped.

Childwork demands the development of this intelligence, to some degree, in all of its workers.

And here is a great weakness in a "materialist" (as we have understood matter in the past) political analysis:

> *Human emotional needs (self-esteem)*
> *are as basic to human survival as food.*

Absolute lack of food results in the death of humans.

Absolute lack of self-esteem results in suicide, the death of humans.

Childworkers know that human infants will cry, wail, writhe in their beds, sicken themselves screaming to a point when they cannot even digest food for emotional needs

with exactly the same intensity

that they cry for food.

This is not conditioned behavior.

This is how all humans are born.
Without food, death by starvation (by degrees, or quickly, depending on the scarcity of food).

Without self-esteem, death by self-destruction (in degrees, by alcoholism, by drugs, by a myriad of self-destructive behaviors, or by the quicker and more conscious expedient of suicide).

It can be argued that there must be food in order for self-esteem to be experienced and therefore food is of the first priority, and that is true,

in a sequential sense

but is not true

in a deferable sequential sense spanning the lifetimes of individual humans and their societies.

The provision of the visible material necessities for the development and maintenance of human life is only a priority of sequence, (and not a long sequence at that), not of magnitude.

These two human needs, for food and self-esteem, for animal energy and human energy, are intimately related drives (evolutionary motion—energy) dynamically interacting with the forces outside of human beings that fulfill or frustrate them. One is not necessarily dominant over the other in humans. Human emotion may be more powerful than the need to eat. Not only can the desire to eat (survive as an animal) be undermined by the lack of self-esteem, and lead to self-destruction, but it can also be consciously superceded by other human desires, not necessarily even immediately related to the individual, as hunger strikers repeatedly prove.

Emotional energy (not the instinct to survive as an individual); human energy, consciously defined and executed by its embodiment, performed the work of Harriet Tubman. Harriet Tubman obviously did not have the benefit of a Marxist analysis of human priorities. For while a striking worker's self-abnegation can be understood in terms of an immediate possibility of better wages, the analysis gets pretty thin when you look at Harriet Tubman; when you look at Nazim Hikmet standing in a trench of human shit singing songs to his torturers.

What we are talking about here is altruistic behavior

which appears (to its bewildered Marxist observers) to be

self

less

behavior.

It's interesting to observe.

It's behavior which doesn't (necessarily) fulfill the economic interests of the individuals who so behave (although it is often related to them); in fact, it often works against their economic interests. At the same time it can be understood as beneficial to the interests of all humanity.

It looks suspiciously like childwork.

·⋞⋟·

Until very recent times, quantitatively, there have been more male political revolutionaries (out there doing battle in the social relations of production) than there have been female revolutionaries. That's not surprising, since women don't have as much time as men, due to the patriarchal division of labor. And it is heartening to see that men are indeed capable of such (apparently) selfless behavior.

But the number of (apparently) self-sacrificing men out there self-sacrificing for anybody on a daily basis is quite low relative to the number of men in existence.

This is not so in the case of women, in whom the patriarchal division of labor has conditioned

sellf

less
behavior.

"non-profit." For the individual.

but profitable to humanity.

Men have never been fully socialized

and although "selfless" behavior emerges in individual men divorced from the social relations of reproduction, it does not emerge very frequently relative to the number of men in existence, and when it does, it most notoriously does not often extend itself to the relations such individuals have with their families.

Women have never been fully socialized

but "selfless" behavior is conditioned into the majority of them by the social relations of reproduction. It isn't random. It doesn't always extend itself to the relations such individuals have outside of their families, but it does so extend itself with far greater frequency than not, at least as far as their communities, as seen in women's unpaid work at all class levels, in schools, churches and neighborhoods, and extends itself even further into politics in a measurable "gender gap."

·❧·

In men, relative to women, this kind of behavior is much less frequent. Revolutionary women and men behaving "selflessly" come from high and middle class backgrounds (Angela Davis, Che Guevara, Fidel Castro, Ho Chi Minh, Ghandi) as well as the lowest (Sojourner Truth, Harriet Tubman, Zapata, Bill Haywood)

and how many others, lesser known

and unknown

persistently, indefatigably

"unsoldout"

working against their immediate or remote

economic (animal) self interests

for the economic and human interests

of all humanity.

Political parties informed by Marxist insights embody a tremendous contradiction, which is that every last one of their members is expected to behave in a self-sacrificing way, a way which does not promise to further the individual's self interest, or the interest of their class or race in any way which will ever necessarily be perceived by them in their lifetimes and in fact, often patently will not. This unspoken requirement is not an arbitrary one because revolutionary political work under the prevailing conditions requires such behavior or it would never get done. And a revolutionary society, one which is significantly better than the one we live in will require this (apparently) unselfish behavior from all of its members.

·⌒⌒·

What I want to say isn't that revolutions can be "sparked" or accomplished by a few "unselfish" individuals, but that such individuals are not "unselfish" at all, that the human self is driven by more than food

all human selves,

that although the behavior of those particular individuals got tangled up in history in such a way that it got recorded and came to the attention of millions of people, it is not even unusual behavior.

When a woman gives the best pieces of meat to her children and husband; when a little boy pushes his baby sister out of the path of a truck and gets hit himself (and I knew such a little boy. His legs had to be amputated.); when a shop clerk works an extra ten minutes so her tired coworker can have a longer break; when a peasant man stands in front of his family (the first to go down) in a confrontation with an army, nothing unusual is going on.

It is interesting that when women behave this way, they identify such behavior as "feminine" (maternal instinct, "womanly, nurturing behavior") and when men behave this way, they identify such behavior with their sex, too: (Brave, "manly"). This is amusing because what it is is human behavior. It gets divided up in our minds because it has been divided up in our labor.

If a little girl had pushed her baby sister out of the way of the truck, it would have been seen as nurturing "little mother" behavior; in a little boy, as "macho."

It is something that transcends her individual self, so it must be her sex.

It is something that transcends his individual self, so it must be his sex.

It is an extraordinarily persistent confusion because the fulfillment of animal needs and the fulfillment of human emotional needs intersect in sexual fulfillment.

In women this commonplace behavior has been channeled forcibly (by the patriarchal division of labor) into childwork which simultaneously elicits, reinforces, and concretizes such behavior to a degree that it has become largely predictable in women.

In men, it's been stunted by their preoccupation with the social relations of production (it's a real jungle out there: you can't afford to be a nice guy); underdeveloped by their isolation from most of humanity; and channeled into all sorts of abstractions such as nationalism, patriotism, religions, philosophies, art, professionalism, science, and politics, with far less predictable benefits for humanity.

Any political theory that focuses on human social organization as it has emerged in consequence of the fulfillment of human animal needs (correctly), and does not focus on (out of ignorance) or ignores (out of fear) or downgrades (out of contempt) "the ultimate cause and great moving power" of human emotional needs impelled by human self-interest, isn't useful at projecting a political order that will empower their fulfillment,

and what's more, embodies an attitude disturbingly familiar to women.

The work which has been assigned (by patriarchy) exclusively to women produces love. Love almost universally emerges in the social relations of reproduction. Real, concrete love. Which everybody, most especially including those threadbare revolutionaries embroidering away on their economic analyses in the world's jails, are looking for.

Real, concrete love.

Produced by real, concrete labor relations.

Women even come to love the men who individually oppress them in this grotesque division of labor, because the very needs women are forced to recognize and fulfill in men belie all the other overwhelming evidence of their inhumanity.

Women are forced to perceive men as human.

Any political theory that downgrades the importance of human emotional needs won't attract or sustain women as it does men, because in the basic industry of fulfilling human emotional needs, women have always been the workers, and women know better.

·❦·

It isn't the case that men must be integrated into the social relations of reproduction only because it will improve their self-esteem in relation to women and children; or because it will condition them into a concrete concern with "other than self"; or because it will empower them with personal self-discipline; or because it will temper their aggression by forcing them to examine and control it; or because it will equip them to recognize and fulfill human emotional needs; or because it will liberate the minds of men from the narrow, stultifying bondage of binary, mechanical, linear thought;

or because childwork will force them into adulthood, precluding the prolonged childhood in which they are nurtured by women from birth to death, by reversing social relations from child to childworker;

or because of the likely transference of "sellf-less" behavior conditioned by childwork into the rest of their social relations with humanity

or because children see through and are notoriously unimpressed with human pretense and police the egos of their workers mercilessly, a service the male ego badly needs, having gone wild and untrimmed for too long. Only children, who do not have the "sense" of their economic interests or any sexual interests at stake, can provide this service;

or because small children are also notoriously uninhibited by class and race and violate such frontiers with their shameless integrity, a contradiction to adult reality which women are exposed to in the streets and playgrounds even in this racially tense society;

not only because men need children,

but because children need men desperately.

·❦·

Before examining the "effects of the internal laws of socialization subject to this lopsided division of labor" which have so deeply aggravated the accumulation of power by men and the subjugation of women, I want to address an ideological issue which critically debilitates much of published feminist thought.

At this time, as in the past, the power (energy) relations inherent in the patriarchal division of labor are so overwhelmingly negative in such an overwhelming number of ways, for all parties involved (children, women and men), that many women, especially the women who have been enabled by their class backgrounds and fierce personal struggle to educate themselves enough to even theorize about this, conclude that most human ills derive from these patriarchal relations, that patriarchy is the primary well of human suffering, and must be addressed before any other form of human oppression can be addressed and/or ever will be redressed.

This line of speculation implies that class oppression and race oppression will fall down go boom as an inevitable consequence of the elimination of patriarchy—or that, at least, they are secondary problems.

Many observations can be made about this idea. One of the most obvious is that indeed patriarchy is the most acutely felt (if not the only) form of oppression directly experienced by some of the women who entertain this idea. This observation is regularly made by progressives and some liberals who then go on to discredit the struggle against patriarchy as either "liberal middle class" and therefore undeserving of serious work, or, more benevolently, secondary to their (more important) work.

The same observation is made as well by some people of color who are working against race oppression, who then go on to discredit the struggle against patriarchy as not only "liberal middle class" but white, undeserving of serious work, or, more benevolently, secondary to their (more important) work.

One of the easiest ways to avoid the legitimate demands made by feminists is to take pot shots at it from behind the barricades of other legitimate struggles any time it lifts its (not always white) head from behind its own.

In reality, all these insurgents against the present order need to willingly unite objectives or be united forcibly in defeat. The fact that some women only seem able to focus on patriarchy is indeed often (mis)informed by their race and class experience, but the phenomenon they are primarily concerned about isn't an "idea"—it's a stark reality unbounded by race or class. It doesn't go away by trivializing the women who articulate it, women who are neither all white or middle class. (The voices of such women who are not white or middle class are not so widely broadcast, for reasons which should be obvious to the other insurgents).

It's important, too, before dismissing the primacy of the struggle against patriarchy to see that, for all women, it does hold a certain truth. And this truth is that women must first liberate themselves as women personally to some extent before they can engage in any political struggle at all. This may be done as "feminists" or done without ever consciously formulating it as a struggle against patriarchy, but women must rescue their self-esteem from the ravages of male domination in order to fight effectively (any fight) and must defy the all-consuming demands on their time that the patriarchal division of labor imposes.

Direct political struggle against racism and against class oppression displaces (in varying degrees, in varying circumstances) the demands of childwork (another worker must be recruited, paid, or forced into an empty shift); housework (shared by others or neglected); ceremonial work (mounting the birthday party, the wedding, quinceañera, bar mitzvah, Ramadan feast); attending the sick (a soothing bath for the five-year-old, laundry for the incontinent elder; disinfecting toilets, taking temperatures, accompaniment to the doctor or curandero); emotional work (an ear for a discouraged husband, visits to the old, lullabies for the baby); producing goods and services which are not profitable (shopping critically, planning menus, preparing and storing food, making up toys or games for children; mending; beautifying; managing and ministering and administering endlessly).

On top of all this, women, like men, have to find time and energy outside of the demands of their jobs in factories, fields, and offices to engage in direct political struggle.

Unlike men, women are frequently so internally oppressed that they also must struggle just to believe in themselves, in their abilities and judgment outside of the work patriarchy has defined for them in order to even consider their contributions to those struggles either worthwhile in themselves or worthwhile undertaking in the first place. So when women say that patriarchy must be dealt with first, there is some truth to it, for women. And that truth extends to men in the measure that men, who are fighting their deeply felt oppressions of class and race, need the political efforts of women to achieve the objectives which the men consider important.

But it is not true that gender oppression is the cause of the others.

The cause of each one is rooted in the history of the whole economy of human survival up to the present and childwork is only one aspect of that economy and its development, albeit a fundamental one. Gender, class, and race dynamics are deeply fused.

Racism, for example, is deeply aggravated by the early amputation of "other relatedness" in the way we rear our young, an amputation which serves as well as an economic prop of slavery and capitalism. Racism deeply supports gender oppression and class division as well. White working class women and men defeat their efforts at unionizing their class with racism and their energies and insights are deeply distorted and misplaced by patriarchal power relations. The exploitation of women of color by men of color within patriarchal power relations creates personal and political discord between them which hampers the unity they need to address race and class oppression.

All these things feed on one another. None of them can be entirely solved in isolation. It isn't only academic at this point, but downright dangerous to assume that if women had had more power, history would have been different. History went on as it did for reasons fairly obvious to us now, not then. Just as our self-extensions (technologies) have turned around and affected us by revolutionizing our economies in entirely unforeseen ways, it is reproductive technology (birth control) that makes possible change in that part of the whole economy of human survival organized at the present time by gender.

None of the genuine insights and objectives of Marxists, feminists, and all people working against racism conflict in reality, unless we prioritize them in isolation from each other. It is always tempting, in trying to make sense of these relations, to attribute to the victims moral superiority over the victimizers. But it is the *position occupied* by those exploited in these decidedly amoral power relations which give the victims an aura of moral superiority, not their humanity.

So women who get all high and mighty over the disastrous stupidities of men and gloss over or ignore their own racism are simply not credible. And men who strut around in political organizations shoving all the domestic work and organizing shitwork off on women whose "issues" they promise to attend "later" are not credible "liberators" either.

The solution to the many divisions which are created around this issue of primacy is to keep the demands for change, and the work for change (and the forbearance for change), as interlocked and inclusive as the oppressions are themselves. I want to say this at the outset because we are going to look now at the subjective, inner effects of patriarchy, and those effects are so universally dehumanizing that they do indeed deeply nourish all other forms of human oppression.

Patriarchy is the result of a human division of the labor necessary to human survival. The core of patriarchy, around which all other patriarchal institutions revolve, is the absolute responsibility of women for primary childwork. This central fact of human life (energy expenditure) has come to give an objective, recognizable "character," ("nature") to women, simply by virtue of the human qualities conditioned into the workers who do such work. Work transforms the worker in specific ways inherent to the work being done.

But the "worked upon" is transformed by this energy expenditure as well; deeply formed and colored by the identity of its worker. The "worked upon" in childwork are all human beings. What this means within the internal laws of human socialization as they are structured by the patriarchal division of labor has a great deal to do with the nature of time.

Time is energy displacing itself.

That is, time has no reality except in relation to energy.

We can infer the "passage" (movement) of geological time (energy) by observing the strata of the earth, for example, but we don't directly "experience" it because our own motion pulses at a much higher frequency, so much higher that the mountains around us appear motionless by comparison.

Astronauts floating outside their capsules in the earth's orbit don't "feel" that they are moving 17,000 miles per hour, because there is no matter (energy) in space dense enough (compared to our bodies) to "feel" it in relation to, but they do indeed move at 17,000 miles per hour.

So although humans have measured the frequency of the earth's movement around the sun and arbitrarily designated that particular frequency as "time," even that "time" is experienced differentially by us, according to our relations with other forms of energy.

Our relations with other forms of energy

form us in a way directly related to this subjective experience of time.

Now there is some law about time which is universally experienced by humans and that is, that the older they get, the faster time seems to pass.

This has to do with accommodation to stimuli (other forms of energy making contact with us).

That is, we get "used to" many of these motions and so direct our conscious energy toward those which are less predictable or more interesting (novel).

Children live in a dimension of time very different from the one adults live in because *everything* is still new, still novel, still unpredictable, interesting, and demanding of serious attention. The famous energy expenditure of children which results in a degree of exhaustion that can send a toddler toppling over her blocks into deep sleep

is the result of coping with the sensory bombardment of

being

indiscriminately.

As time goes on, the fact that ants appear and move over the surface of things; the fact that rain falls and shadows move and hair tangles and food is slippery and urine fills the bladder, hot burns, moon shines, glass breaks and an infinity of even smaller events which children notice

are moved into the unconscious,

which saves a great deal of conscious energy,

and which, simultaneously, speeds up the *experience* of time.

It's important to keep this in mind when exploring the effects of childhood socialization because we have the most prolonged infancy of any mammal species. We remain helpless to survive without adults for years, not just for months. These two facts, the fact of our extremely prolonged childhood, and our temporal experience of that childhood which gives it a subjective existence in our formation almost equal to the duration of the rest of our lives, give the circumstances of our socialization into adult humanity a degree of power (energy) to influence our formation, out of proportion to the "objective" length of time we exist.

It's no accident or mystery that children will (apparently) effortlessly absorb two languages simultaneously while they occupy this all-stimuli-absorbing dimension of time, but rarely can repeat the same achievement in adulthood without immense effort, and even then may never achieve the same degree of virtuosity. We are never so impressionable again. Outside of severe adult traumas, the "impressions" imprinted on our on-going formation are never again so deep or so durable.

It's during this period, the same period during which we master the infinitely complex structures of language, that we are gendered. And dealing with gender, later, is like trying to extirpate a language, the vehicle of a culture so deeply embedded in prerational experience that our very identities, our sense of ourselves, of security, of our self esteem are welded into it at levels rarely investigated by—and therefore increasingly inaccessible to—that latecomer, "reason," which builds its burgeoning constructions over those unexamined foundations.

Now it's obviously not true that all human problems derive from our childhood conditioning, or that deformities in our humanity that do result from childhood conditioning are immune to some degree of change in the course of soul-wrenching human events and/or soul-wrenching, conscious human efforts to change the results of that conditioning, for "growing up" is a continuum, not an event. But the power of that conditioning to frustrate human growth, to slow or arrest it on that continuum along which many developments move at different speeds throughout our lifetimes (if they ever move at all—are ever allowed birth) is immense. That power shouldn't be underestimated, but frequently is by the very people who are struggling intensely to structure reason into other parts of the economy of human survival before it self-destructs.

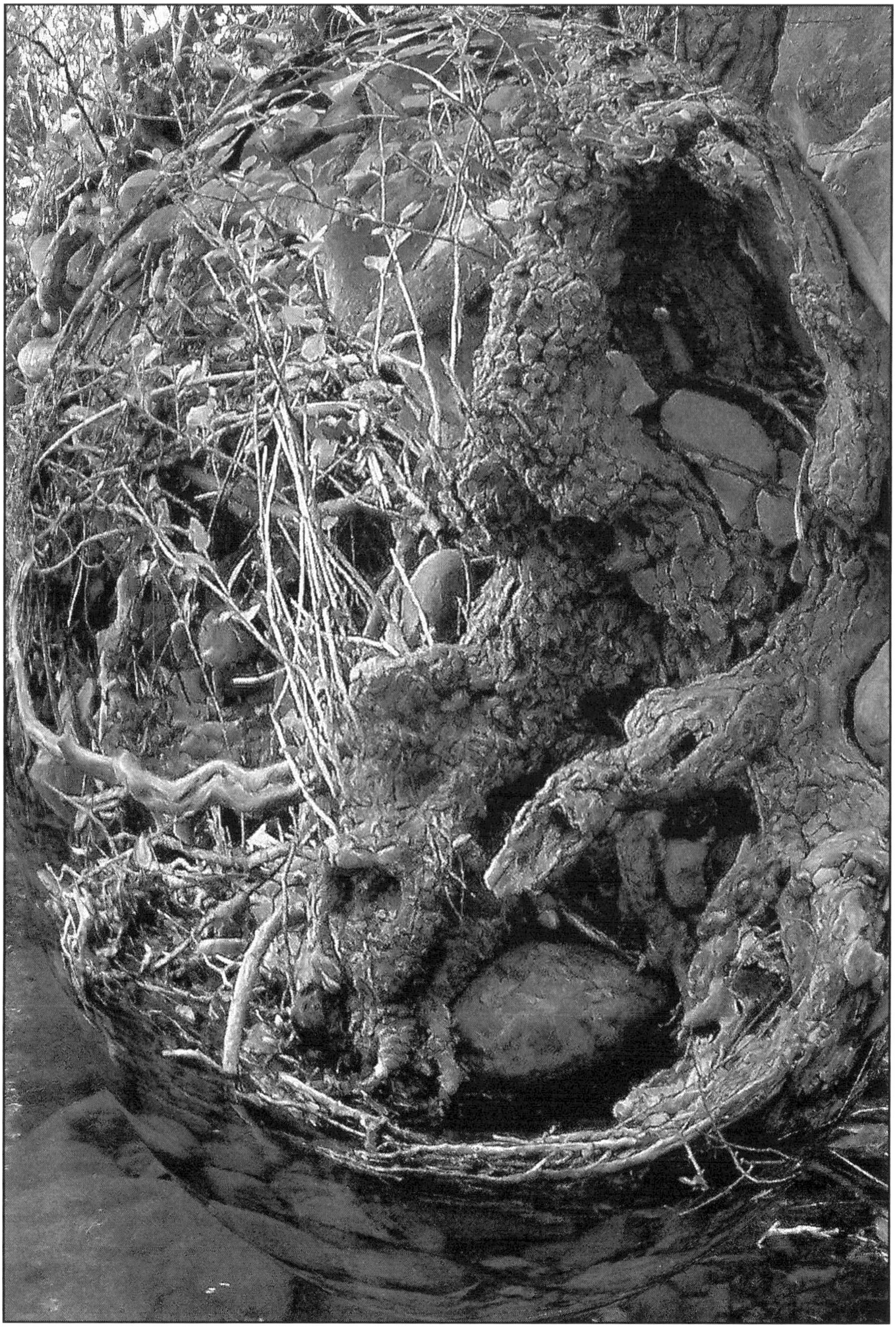

CHAPTER IV

The All-Powerful Female

Our integration into the power relations of human social organization is enforced by women. It's accomplished under circumstances in which female power is experienced as omniscient and sometimes terrifying, as we are born so helpless, and remain so helpless for so long (nearly half of our subjective lives), that every pleasure, pain, relief from pain, opportunity, frustration, achievement, failure—most self-esteem and humiliation—spring from or are dependent on female power.

This female power elicits soulrending shrieks of bottomless fear if it is absent, if it does not respond. Dorothy Dinnerstein writes:

> The earliest roots of antagonism to women lie in the period before the infant has any clear idea where the self ends and the outside world begins...At this stage a woman is the helpless child's main contact with the natural surround, the center of everything the infant wants and feels drawn to, fears losing and feels threatened by. She is the center also of the non-self, an unbounded, still unarticulated region within which the child labors to define itself.... She is this global, inchoate, all-embracing presence before she is a person...
>
> When she does become a person, her person-ness is shot through for the child with these earlier qualities...
>
> One result of female dominated child care, then, is that the trouble every child has in coming to see that the magic parental presence of infancy was human, a person, can be permanently side-stepped: women can be defined as quasi persons, quasi humans; and unqualified human personhood can be sealed off from the contaminating atmosphere of infant fantasy and defined as male. (93)

This antagonism has its "earliest roots" in infancy, but blows up into an ever more conscious *prerational* struggle throughout the toddler years and into childhood, because the all-powerful female is differentiated from ourselves fairly early on. We experience her power as not only universal, but capricious: that is, attached to a female will. She's not only the source of affection, food, amusement, comfort, but, in their absence, perceived as the *source* of their denial, the source of all pain and humiliation.

Dinnerstein notes, as all mothers note, that "...the human infant's intelligence makes the gap between what it can actually do and what it can think of doing immense." Dinnerstein is looking, stunned, at the obvious. And she brings it to our attention: "... it is woman who presides alone over this self-discovery of the proud, active, and enragingly puny flesh" (132).

I would add that not only the human infant's intelligence, but the human child's and even adolescent's intelligence "makes the gap between what it can actually do and what it can think of doing immense."

This fact is the most salient feature of the difficult work of the childworker. Human children are not only helpless outside the womb far longer than other mammals, but are endowed with this burgeoning, problematic human consciousness. They require so much childwork precisely because, from infancy on up, they can conceive of doing (and urgently desire to do) much more than their slower developing bodies (and body of experience) permit.

This human condition is the source of endless conflict between child and childworker. It is deeply, consistently humiliating to the child, and deeply, consistently stressful to the childworker. It's this enormous body of accumulated pain and humiliation that we push as far out of our memories as possible as we emerge from childhood. We create a collective myth about childhood to protect us from those memories and their associated pain and rage, for the rest of our lives. This is the myth of the "idyllic" childhood; childhood as teddy bears and twinky twinky stars; of doting adults and huggy mommies; of carefree romps through the numinous (non-polluted) fields and forests.

In fact, we even project this infantile nostalgia on real children around us, much to their confusion and consternation, talking about doggies and horsies; assuming that they want our compulsive hugs as badly as we want the solace of their fresh bodies; staring at them or talking about them as though they were not self-conscious. Children don't have these illusions about childhood. They don't want to be children. They want to be grown up.

It is true that we sometimes stay in touch with some fragmentary memories of the wonder (not the terror), spontaneity (which we like to remember as unimpeded but which was impeded, at every turn) and delicious pleasures of childhood (much the same as our pleasures now, just fresher and unmodified by a sense of responsibility), but we most decidedly don't stay in touch with the feelings of rage, burning humiliation, greed and vengefulness that we accumulated simultaneously. All those feelings are shunted far off into the unconscious, where they remain, unrecognized but very much alive.

There's a great pathos in watching an infant of one month struggle, red-faced, with the effort to roll over. The fact is, she can't roll over and this fact is never accepted (fortunately), but the effort is accompanied with cries of frustration over and over and over. We do eventually roll over. The efforts end in triumph. But the triumph was preceded by painful struggle, by a long string of humiliations which are not "forgotten," but are as real to us and as deeply lodged in our memories as the childworker's support and comfort which those efforts simultaneously demanded.

The ability to lift the head, roll over, crawl, walk, eat unaided, button a shirt, belong to a category of achievements which are assured, after intense struggle and repeated, deeply resented defeats, success. They exhaust both child and childworker for years, but at least the objectives of both are in accord during the process.

But this is the least of it, because childworkers are, much of the time, directly opposed to children's desires. The irrationality and ignorance of children are the source of far more work for childworkers than children's struggles with physical incompetence.

Here's an example from a context with a refrigerator in it. (But of course, this dilemma is repeated with fabulous variation in every economic and cultural context known to humans).

The childworker freezes juice into bars the two and a half year old can suck and calm her aching molars on. The freezer is low and the child can reach them.

It's a source of pride that one can go to the freezer unaided and get one of those bars without adult interference. This privilege, like each privilege in its turn, is a jealously defended symbol of much desired selfhood: independence.

But today the childworker was late in putting in the bars, so they are liquid.

The child confidently approaches the freezer.

The childworker foresees the big messy event about to occur and forbids the child the bar of juice.

Now it's not just hunger at work here. It's not just a toothache. It's much, much more.

It's the integrity of the self.

Stunned by yet another arbitrary adult violation to justice and freedom,

the child insists.

Is refused.

All the defenses of the self are mustered up for battle.

The child persists.

The situation deteriorates into a physical struggle and the child is now shouting.

The childworker takes apart the plastic case and shows the child that it is only liquid; explains (knowing full well the explanation will not be understood but moved by a sense of human justice as well as the obligation of a childworker to repeat many things until learned or believed) that it is not frozen. That the child can have a bar later.

Now, "later" is a very abstract concept between two people who don't live in the same time dimension.

Moreover, the child knows nothing about the properties of liquid in a freezer. The child knows that there are supposed to be bars in there (for the child); that somehow the bars are ruined. That this, like every other unpleasantness in life, is the childworker's fault.

Insult is added to deep injury.

The child fights for freedom and justice and propriety.

The child is integral and all the power of this integrity is brought to bear on this unbearable situation.

The child screams for the bar, lunges into the freezer.

The childworker (fast, as childworkers are forced to be, hurting for the hurt in the child, resenting the impossible demand of the child, nerves raw from the implacable crying, and undoubtedly pressured to attend to other work)

rescues the tray of bars just in the nick

and puts them on top of the refrigerator,

out of the child's reach!

The child now experiences the behavior of the childworker as not only unreasonable, not only unjust and wounding, but vicious! A vicious, hideous, unprovoked attack on the reasonableness, competence, and integrity of the child.

The child's pain and frustration border on apoplexy. Her outraged face is mottled; she gasps between screams; hot tears burst from her immense grief.

She may rush up and pummel her fists on the childworker. She may throw her little body on the floor, sobbing and shrieking. Some children will hold their breath in an almost suicidal rage against their own helplessness; or will grab and smash whatever is at hand in impotent fury.

This, too, is childhood.

If you're a childworker and you look into the eyes of a child at such times (and those times are frequent, much more frequent than either party can bear to remember), what you will see there isn't only pain that strikes through your heart, but livid hatred.

Hatred invested with the emotional purity of a child.

The purest, most undisguised hatred you will ever be the object of.

Hatred accompanied by a searing desire for vengeance.

·⌒☙⌒·

You might say, well, the childworker should have just let the child have a go at the bars. However, this would not abate the child's anger that the bars are not there. In fact, it might well exacerbate it. Secondly, the ensuing child/bar engagement could well occupy hours in accumulated laundry, clothes-changing, bathing, floor mopping, freezer cleaning.

So you might say, well, the childworker could have avoided this situation by having the bars in there on time. And indeed, a great deal of childwork is composed of the (invisible) intellectual and physical effort to foresee and forestall just such events,

events peculiar at any given time to the constantly expanding, ever more complicated state of the child's development, but outwitting them all of the time is just plain impossible.

·⌒☙⌒·

Maya Angelou, who performed her childwork with great sensitivity, records this in a context with a car in it.

> She and her seven year old son, Guy, were riding as passengers in the family truck one morning in San Francisco. Her husband Tosh was driving. At an intersection there was an accident Tosh was unable to avoid and she was thrown forward into the windshield, her teeth crushed on the dashboard:
>
>> When I regained consciousness, Tosh was blowing his breath in my face and murmuring. I asked about Guy and Tosh said that as the car hit, I grabbed for Guy and folded him in my arms. Now he was standing on the corner unhurt.
>> I got out of the truck and walked over to my son, who was being consoled by strangers. When I bent down at his side, he took one glance at my battered face and instead of coming into my arms, he began to scream, strike out at me and back away.
>> Tosh had to come to talk him into the taxi. For days, he moped around the house avoiding my gaze. Each time I turned quickly enough to catch him looking at me, I shivered at the hateful accusation in his eyes.
>> We had not caused the accident. Tosh had been the driver, and I was the most injured person. But I was the mother, the most powerful person in his world who could make everything better. Why had I made them worse? I could have prevented the accident. I should not have allowed our truck to be at that place at that time. If I hadn't been so neglectful, my face would not have been cut, my teeth would not be broken and he would not have been scared out of his wits.
>> Now, eight years later, Guy was asking himself why had I, by neglecting my duty, why had I put his pride in jeopardy? Had I thought that being married removed my responsibility to keep the world on its axis and the universe in order? (247)

These feelings are almost always felt about women. It's women who wrong us. Who violate our integrity. Who attack us with their arbitrary, despotic, vicious authority. And our vengeance is unrequited. All this desire to get back at women (the childworkers) for the intense humiliations they, and they alone inflict upon us, has to go underground because it's neither acceptable nor possible to enact.

It has to go underground because it doesn't go away. It doesn't go away any more than our love for our childworker ever goes away. And because those emotions are so painful to admit and impossible to follow through, they remain far more unmodified throughout our lifetimes than do other emotions. Our feelings of love for her get air, are exercised for what they are because they are acceptable. But our spite against women cankers away behind masks. We ourselves don't recognize it for what it is. Women, Dinnerstein observes,

> ...bear the brunt of a profound, many-faceted early filial spite, and they bear it alone. If this spite were directed simply at parents, not just female parents (and

subsequently at their gender as a whole), it could be more consciously identified for what it is—a childish, outgrowable feeling—and endured, forgiven. But under prevailing conditions it is impossible to forgive, and too painful to be squarely identified, because although it is childish it is never outgrown: the availability of woman as target makes outgrowing it unnecessary. Women meet it not only in their children but in the world at large. They start meeting it long before they are mothers. It is a pervasive societal motif. (173-174)

·꒰ঌ·

The reach of a child's consciousness is so inverse to a child's ignorance for such a long time, and the complexities of the world so great and unpredictable (and often unavoidable even if they are predictable), that intense conflict between child and childworker are the very stuff of daily, hourly childwork,

just as are love, wonder, solidarity and delight

(the things we prefer to remember).

If that weren't enough, there are times (also frequent), when children actually create such situations (and children are very imaginative about this)

purposefully,

to test themselves in relation to you, the childworker,

just to see how things are going.

Women embody the energy children experience themselves (and measure themselves)

in relation to.

And of course, for years, they don't measure up. Cannot surpass.

And resent the childworker again.

But they keep trying to "win"

every test of will.

In the patriarchal divison of labor, getting the hell away from women,

putting women behind you,

and ah, yes
at last,

dominating women

in turn

constitute the achievement of selfhood,

the achievement of humanity itself.

·⊱⊰·

The female is so all-powerful, in relation to children—in the objective and subjective experience of children—that women become deeply identified with nature itself.

"Female sentience," Dinnerstein writes,

> carries permanently for most of us the atmosphere of that unbounded, shadowy presence toward which all our needs were originally directed. And the intentionality that resides in female sentience comes in this way to carry an atmosphere of the rampant and limitless, the alien and unknowable. It is an intentionality that needs to be conquered and tamed, corralled and subjugated, if we (men most urgently, but women too) are to feel at all safe in its neighborhood. (164)

and: "Woman is the will's first, overwhelming adversary....In our first real contests of will, we find ourselves, more often than not, defeated: the defeat is always intimately carnal; and the victor is always female" (166).

Our relations with this female power and will are drenched with a terrible ambivalence. We need and desire her passionately, yet female forbids us, *forbids* us: the desired toy (we do not know "she" is poor); the embrace of the shining slippery silvery (river); the hot tortilla (on the fire); the fascinating yellow eyed furry (cat); access to the luxurious place (for whites).

Female ignores us (we don't know that "she" must work)

Female splatters us with blood and pain ("she" didn't prevent us from falling down)

Female forces from our hands the cool smooth power object (knife)

Female closes boxes, shuts drawers, removes objects of tantalizing beauty and interest

    Female hurt our arms dressing us

    Female forced us into unpleasant tasks cleaning up after ourselves

    Female forced us inside, out of the sweet wet fragrant drop rush

    Female hurt our head untangling hair

    Female didn't prevent the death and loss of our dog, fish, grandmother, innocence at every level

    Female saw us bawl, fall, dirty ourselves, spill things, fail

    Female has been the devastating witness to all our failures; knows our weaknesses with crushing intimacy, in crushing detail

    Female even has the gall to *predict* them

    Female "told us so"

    Female controls the food we do or don't eat, the hours we eat it, the hours we sleep, the places we can and cannot go, what we wear, who we see, what we do

    Female hurt us with the sharp words

    Female misunderstood us (most early and most often)

    Female betrayed us by telling others (including remote males)

    Female jailed us off from the excitement by putting us to bed

    Female is an obstacle, a threat, an engulfing monster, the enemy of our (in the human species chronically premature) attempts to be independent

    Female is most beloved being in the universe

    and at the same time, the object of the most intense rage, greed, and livid resentment we ever experience. But kick, flail, scream, pout, burn with humiliation as we will, vengeance is frustrated. Female dominates.

    Female dominates for years.

Now, as we emerge into the world having known nothing but the domination of women during many intensely vulnerable years which span a huge portion of our subjective life(times), how are we supposed to *feel* about women?

"The crucial psychological fact is that all of us, female as well as male, fear the will of woman," Dinnerstein writes. In consequence,

> So long as the first parent is a woman, then woman will inevitably be pressed into the dual role of indispensable quasi-human supporter and deadly quasi-human enemy of the human self. She will be seen as naturally fit to nurture other people's individuality; as the born audience in whose awareness other people's subjective existence can be mirrored; as the being so peculiarly needed to confirm other people's worth, power, significance that if she fails to render them this service she is a monster, anomalous and useless. At the same time she will also be seen as the one who will not let other people be, the one who beckons her loved ones back from selfhood, who wants to engulf, dissolve, drown, suffocate them as autonomous persons. (111)

> The possibility that a man will interrupt a woman's train of thought, interfere with her work, encourage her to sink back into passivity, make her an appendage of himself, does not engender the same panic in most of us as the possibility that she will do this to him. The original threat that we all felt in this connection was felt as emanating from a woman, and we lean over backward in our heterosexual arrangements to keep this original threat at bay. We will have to continue to do so, in some way, until we reorganize child care to make the realm of the early non-self as much a male as a female domain. (112)

The consequences of the patriarchal division of labor which spiral out of this early, unilateral power relation are massive structural reinforcements to the survival of that power arrangement. The reinforcements resonate with such harmonic frequency that the whole arrangement seems "natural." We experience the consequences differentially, either as men or as women, but they mutilate the humanity of us both.

Dinnerstein describes (and many other women have described this) the destructive phenomenon of identifying women (exclusively women) with nature (woman as earth; man as "cultivator"), by which we come to project on women (and only women) the powerful feelings we have about mortality itself; about the flesh which is going to betray us into death (non-selfhood) at the end. She describes the intermediate, psychologically crippling effects as we gender ourselves in imitation of the same-sex parent, as children whose "first extended encounter is with a woman, rather than with both a woman *and* a man," a fact which

> makes it in some ways harder to become a woman than a man. At the same time, it makes men in some ways more helpless with women than women are with men. The woman feels herself on the one hand a supernatural being, before whom the

man bluffs, quails, struts, and turns stony for fear of melting; and she feels herself on the other hand a timid child, unable to locate in herself the full magic power which as a baby she felt in her mother. The man can seem to her to fit her childhood ideal of a male adult far better than she herself fits her childhood ideal of a female adult. This flaw in her sense of inner authority deepens from within a feeling of hers which society at the same time abundantly encourages from the outside: that she is unqualified for full worldly adult status... (85-86)

"What we have worked out," she wryly notes, "is a masquerade, in which generation after generation of childishly self-important men on the one hand, and childishly play-acting women on the other, solemnly recreate a child's-eye view of what adult life must be like" (87).

The internal dynamics of these feelings about women reverberate in our objective experience, corroding and degrading our lives in ways documented in devastating variation by a growing body of women's literature. These include the greedy, infantile violence of rape, vibrating up a scale from smirks and leers to stabbing, disembowelment, decapitation; the masochism of women and the sadism of men, with all their under and overtones; the monstrous segregation of our humanity into two gender cultures and the alienation so achieved; the ironic infantilization of women, for they must be made, even in appearance, childlike for us to be adult "in relation to" (and victimlike to complete our fantasies); social relations between the sexes so poisoned that love itself is defined as a "battleground."

These are the fruits of the patriarchal division of labor, of children

abandoned by men.

·☙·

This is very hard stuff to digest,

because while it's all very well to look at an objective analysis of the patriarchal division of labor and see how it has forced on women qualities of self-discipline, endurance, emotional insight, patience, and so on, it isn't so easy to come to terms with Dinnerstein's revolutionary analysis of the internal dynamics of the patriarchal division of labor, because it hurts. It attacks the sense we have of ourselves as women, the shaky esteem for ourselves as women which patriarchy has substituted for the real thing.

·☙·

Patriarchal ideology (necessarily!) romanticizes children. Our sense of unassailable importance in the patriarchal scheme of things is based on denying the humanity of children, who are supposed to be seen in a way which is even more ridiculous, demeaning, and stultifying than the patriarchal view of women.

We are supposed to see children as tender, loving, wise little creatures endowed with supernatural goodness and sweetness which we, as women, sacrifice our very lives to protect.

This serves to make women feel very noble about themselves. We are crushed, but crushed in a good cause. We are martyred on the maternal altar but we throw ourselves upon it in the name of all that is good, beautiful, and tender.

   Children.

   Innocent angels.

   Patriarchal ideology refuses to describe children as human.

   The distinction between "good" and "bad" is not something they are born with. A child in control of a toy may be, for quite awhile, just as inclined to hit another child who also desires it as to share it. Children are sometimes violent and greedy. Sometimes they are vengeful and mean.

Their violence, greed, vengefulness and egotism are not merely products of bad upbringing (the fault of women!), or even aberrations of human development that they "grow out of" like fontanels and wisdom teeth, but are universal human feelings which are guided and checked only by acquiring the knowledge that, unguided and unchecked, they are not in our interest.

The honesty (integrity; wholeness) of children reveals their human nature, and child-workers are treated to firework displays of human beauty and human intelligence every working day. That same honesty reveals, undisguised, human greed, violence, egotism with the same unselfconscious integrity.

It is patriarchy which asks women to name these qualities "childish." In fact, we go on wrestling with them throughout our adult lives both inside and outside of ourselves.

I think that the anger which can move us to use physical force can also rebuild the world, and that our bottomless desire for pleasure can be harnessed into the struggle to preserve the waterfalls, forests, oceans, the sexuality of women.

   Revolutions emerge out of conflicted energy.

   Children embody all forces we must reckon with to evolve. And just as we need to humanize rather than romanticize them, we need to stop seeing ourselves as the "noble protectors" of children, women whose supposed great moral integrity derives from the supposed great moral integrity of children, and face the fact that they are human,

that we have been forced into a position of unilateral dominance over them,

and human beings do not like to be dominated.

·◈·

If you ask a childworker (almost always, under present gender arrangements, a mother) about "her" children and "her" experience with them, she will always tell you how wonderful they are. She might concede that it is (vaguely) "hard" at times, but mostly she will emphasize how wonderful they are

and she is not lying,

but she never tells the whole truth because the whole truth is not acceptable; it is something she deals with in silence, alone, struggles with in herself,

because if children are all so sweet and beautiful and rewarding as everyone, even her own mother, always has assured her that they are

and she is struggling with these awful displays of hatred and episodes of destructiveness in *her* children, (displays, moreover, frequently and unmistakably directed at *her*), there must be something wrong with *her*.

And she knows there is. She knows her mothering is deficient. All mothers know it. She tries and tries but selfishness and vengeance keep emerging in her children despite everything. They were "perfect" when they were born and she knows she is the one "ruining" them, knows well her absolute position of authority in relation to them every day where their primal beauty and perfection are sullied.

Projecting an image of children as unblemished beings is necessary in order to preserve women's guilt and self-hatred. Both are experienced with such intense subjectivity that the women around the sandbox leap to the rescue of the child who is about to have his eye gouged with a plastic shovel and force the children apart

without ever really talking about it.

It is done with annoyance and exasperation and always

apologetically

by the mother of the offending child,

often with an excuse: "He's teething. He's tired. He's been upset since we moved. This isn't typical of him at all."

(Crying inside *He isn't like this. He is really beautiful. This is not the real child. I know the real child*)

(Crying inside *You are so beautiful. You were born so beautiful. It must be my fault. I try so hard to be a good mother and I know that children are good, good*)

I've watched the condescending patience of the mothers whose children *at that moment* are not being destructive or murderous.

"We know how it is. They all eventually learn to share. Johnny gets tired sometimes, too. Don't worry about it."

Spoken or unspoken.

Watched the secret warmth creep into the breasts of the mothers whose children are not at that moment behaving that way because for that moment their false (patriarchal) self-esteem is nourished. It "tells" them they are good mothers. They are doing a good job,

at least in relation to someone else

at least for that moment.

We talk about the wonderful things the children do and say. We commiserate on their fantastic unreasonableness (so cute, after all), but nobody mentions the murderous violence even in its presence. It is forbidden to talk about.

·⌒⌒·

Women enforce our collective guilt and self-hatred on each other with rigorous cruelty. Thus it is that every woman alive, even if she has never been a childworker, recognizes what a "bad" childworker is: one who ruins the perfection of children! Since children are perfect, they can only be ruined by "interfering" with them.

There are even some feminists, whose thinking is clear and advanced in other ways, who still cannot give up the contempt they nourish for childworkers (women) (and themselves by extension), like Shulamith Firestone, who insisted that "The best way to raise a child is to LAY OFF" (91).

If we leave them alone, they will turn out fine.

    Now it is true that the lie that children are perfect does indeed produce desperate behavior toward them by women who are blamed for the destructive humanity of children, and who are thus charged with molding children to that lie while confronted with real human children day in and day out. And children are interfered with destructively as their workers frantically try to do the impossible, but leaving them alone *is* impossible.

Only men "leave them alone."

Left alone, the child will stick his fingers in the toaster; drop her brother on his head on the sidewalk; drown in the irrigation canal; get drunk, take the car keys, and murder a carload of people.

Childwork *demands* interference.

I would like to see Shulamith Firestone have the responsibility (real fulltime eighteen year responsibility) for a real child, and leave that child alone.

Non-interference, whether it comes in the form of abandonment or just giving a child everything she wants in a nihilistic escape from responsibility to engage in the conflicts of childwork ("spoiling")

    are both experienced

    quite justifiably

    as hatred

    by the children so "left alone."

In fact, it would be a humorous (or sad) spectacle because the child would resist. Children demand the involvement of their workers even when their workers would very, very much like to be "left alone" themselves.

Children do not subscribe to the "You do your thing; I'll do my thing" form of white middle class 20th century alienation reflected in that kind of thinking.

Unexamined in that kind of thinking (and in its other form, "She doesn't interfere enough!") is exactly what Dinnerstein was talking about: contempt for childworkers. Contempt for women. Contempt for the "All Powerful Female" abusing the selfhood of sweet innocent children with her vicious authority, sullying their beauty.

Any attempt with another woman, childworker or not, to examine the real humanity of children, including violence and greed and legendary cruelty, is risky, likely to result in a personal attack, overt or covert:

"It must be *her* experience with *her* children. Children are beautiful. Children are not so bad. *She* must be having a bad time handling *her* responsibility. What is *she* doing to her poor kid that is producing these conflicts? My Johnny doesn't do that kind of thing. Very much. Just when he's teething or tired or upset or..."

No wonder we are silent. We deny the savagery in children as hotly as we deny it in our (personal) selves.

No wonder we are silent, as the full, uncompromised, unDisneyfied, unconcealed, unconditioned, unsocialized, untamed maelstrom of natural forces embodied in the human consciousness and behavior of children unfold before our amazed (and often terrified) eyes.

·~~·

Women bridle at hearing "their" sacred work referred to as "dominating" children. "Dominating" implies a malicious tyrant, not a loving woman. And we do love our children. Oh, how we love them.

But domination is a position in a relationship, not an attitude: a position in a relationship between the powerful and the powerless.

An exploration of the domination of women by men is impossible without exploring the domination of children by women. Indeed, the domination of women by men is incomprehensible in any other context.

Patriarchy isn't merely a system in which men are undersocialized; it is a system in which men rape at least one woman out of every three born; in which men shove their fingers, their penises, and other objects into the vaginas of little girls, or force the mouths of one out of every four little girl children choking over their "manhood"; where women are battered in one of every five homes; where women's labor is spit on with the lowest wages, if any at all.

The coldness and emotional stupidity reflected in such behavior can be understood as a result of undersocialization, but not the *hatred*; not the contempt for women spilling out of the eyes of men over the most trivial conflicts: over washing a cup or questioning a decision, any decision made by a man, so that there is not a woman alive who has never confronted it

who has not been shocked or bewildered by it

who has never recoiled from that hatred which escapes their "cool" exteriors, asking herself in bloody amazement what she ever did to merit it?

Patriarchy is not merely a system in which men are undersocialized; it is a system which breeds specific hatred of women. And when we realize that this infantile hatred, violence, and greed toward women emerges out of a childhood relationship with them (a relationship in which women are as helplessly thrust into the role of powerful as children are helplessly thrust into the role of powerless),

we are forced to realize that our childhood relationship with women was much the same;

that we, too,

were formed

by measuring ourselves against women;

against powerful female authority

which we experienced with the psychology of the powerless

and the unmodified ignorance of children.

We are forced to examine how we, too, have internalized contempt for women,

contempt for ourselves,

because our acquiescence holds the system in place.

Men alone cannot control us.

We must control ourselves.

Hate ourselves.

Dinnerstein's insight is painful because it makes us look at *our* responsibility for patriarchy.

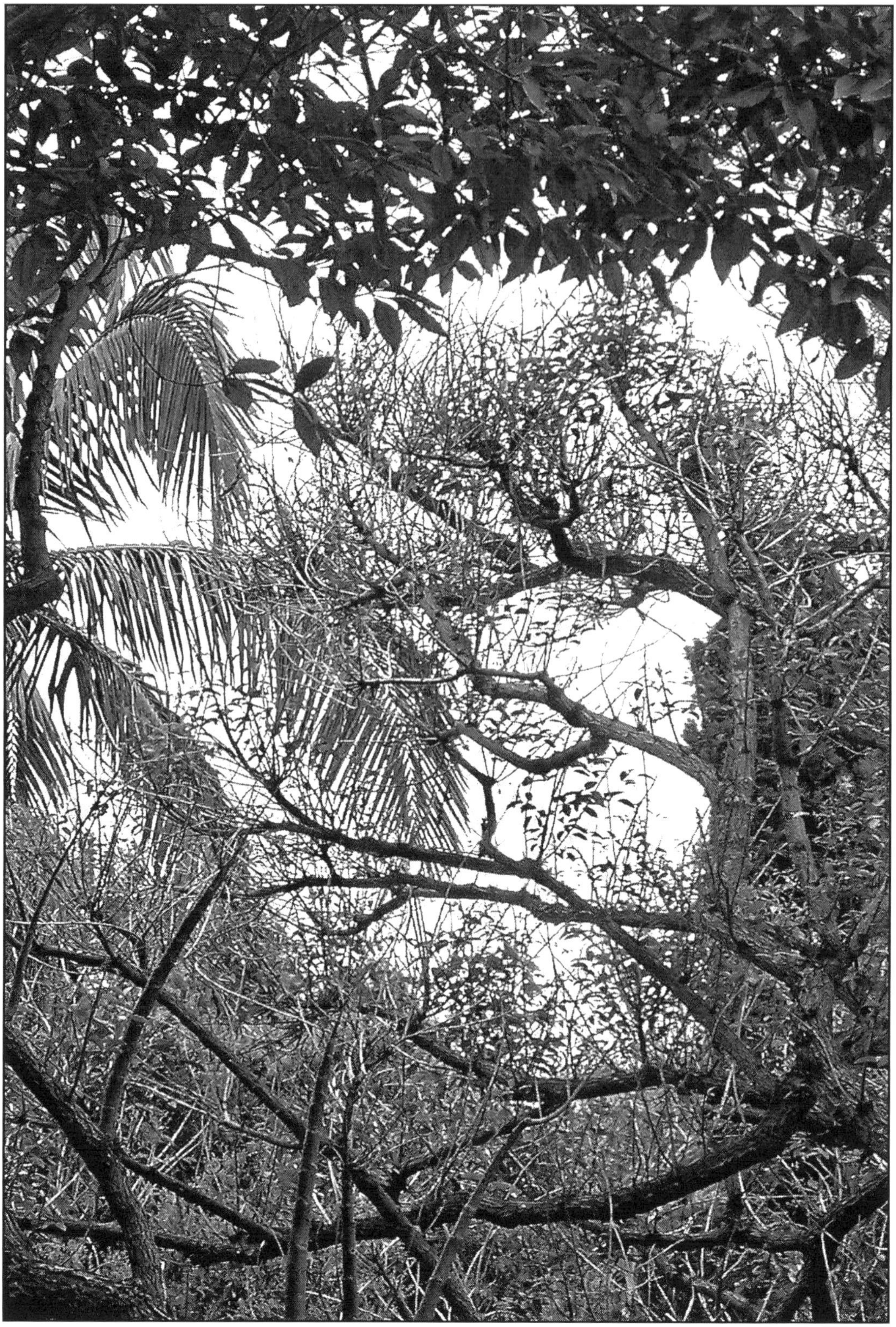

CHAPTER V

The All Powerful Female from Another Angle

"Liberalism has a large number of points for women's equality. The Nazi programme for women has but one: this is the child. While man makes his supreme sacrifice on the field of battle, woman fights her supreme battle for her nation when she gives life to a child." (Hitler)

"Everything, from the baby's first story-book to the last newspaper, theatre, cinema...will be put to this end...until the brain of the tiniest child is penetrated by the glowing prayer: Almighty God, bless our weapons again...bless our battle." (Hitler)

"And is it something inferior to form the soul of a child than to write a book or to accomplish some piece of work?" (Hitler)

☙❧

I think it's worthwhile to look into Hitler's philosophy of gender roles because it might be constructive for many otherwise revolutionary people to learn how closely it parallels their own.

I'm not referring only to the tokenism of white males in political organizations who will shove into conspicuous "positions" only women who disown all political theory other than that of white males; who demean feminism as liberal; or those black men whose political advice to black women at one time was to give up the pill; or Palestinian men who pressured their women to bear children in refugee camps

or any people threatened with genocide who can be confused into thinking that the struggle against genocide can be resolved with the bodies of women when there is no way it can ever be resolved without the minds of those women.

I'm referring to a pervasive idea about the social relations of reproduction which might be called the "blank slate" theory of childhood.

This is the "penetrate the brain of the tiniest child," "form the soul of a child," "woman the shaper, the hewer, the molder of men" number, tricked out in the clothes of whatever ideology is on stage, to warm up the audience for whatever the Big Act is that will permit women to mold, shape, and hew those little up and coming actors in the wings.

Mold, mold, mold.

Shape, shape, shape.

Hew, hew, hew.

Now, if this is the case, how is it that we are so incompetent that we produce all these men who hold us in contempt?

You would think we might hew a little respect into those infantile minds while we were at it.

What happens in reality is that children mold, shape, and hew away at their childworkers;

what happens in reality is that children already *have* souls and find themselves locked into a desperate struggle to protect them,

that children do not need to be reared, they need childworkers to help them rear themselves.

What happens in reality is that children see right through this big blur of molding, shaping, and hewing

and look directly in front of them with those big unfooled eyes,

and see a woman.

·⊱⊰·

The essence of the relationship between child and childworker is separation. Sandra Harding has explored how this is so and developed important insights into the consequences.

Early on, babies don't realize they are separate beings, but this doesn't last long as they stretch out and rear up and take possession of themselves. A long dialectic gets established between the child and the childworker which is a motion away from her; then back for support and reassurance; away from her a little farther; back for support and reassurance.

This dialectic is especially dramatic during the period ending with infancy (when they get mobile) on to about three years of age.

It's a critical period. During this time it dawns fully on the child that she or he is indeed separate, and this is communicated to the childworker roundly and unequivocally with the word "No!"

They discover they can say "No!"

They discover that they are somebody, too.

This is pretty heady stuff, self-discovery. It involves a lot of work, this "psychological birth" because children discover that their own ideas and desires are frequently in conflict with the childworker's.

> The initial, horrible discoveries that humans are imperfect, that they have wills of their own, that they frustrate our projects—this discovery has been made about a woman, about the person on whom we were dependent for survival, about the person from whom we were having difficulty distinguishing and separating ourselves; and the discoveries were made before we had learned to deal with life rationally (Sandra Harding, 151).

Harding describes how it is during this critical period that children discover their bodies, and discover that they are like, or different from, the childworker's. This is when children are gendered. At three years of age they will identify themselves quite loudly, in no uncertain terms, "I'm a girl, not a boy!" "I'm a boy, not a girl!" Most importantly, she notes that gender is not value free.

> For all the hewing and the shaping, there are only two basic molds in the political gender prison children are born into, and they can't even choose between those.
> Gender, she reminds us, is not value free.

The person from whom children individuate, against whom they measure their physical similarities and differences and all the cultural significance attached to those differences or similarities,

is a devalued woman.

More often than not, a woman who is not only objectively devalued, whose labor is devalued, but who has been conditioned to devalue herself.

More often than not, a woman who is tired most of the time, frustrated in many dimensions, and constantly distracted by an endless round of shitwork which must be attended to simultaneous to her relations with these emerging humans.

Where are the men?

Men are remote. Men are physically absent most of the time. The heavy dramas of every day go down with devalued women.

Women are responsible for children.

(A Responsible Aside...)

We all know that that man was a murderer because his mother left him when he was a child.

We all know that every deranged nut who mutilates girls or fires randomly into crowds

had bad relations with his mother.

And if we don't know, the newspaper accounts will inform us.

The newspaper reporters will go around the neighborbood and get unbiased opinions outside of the family

and they are always given pretty straightforward accounts of the childhood of nut X, which, as it happened, was overseen by

a woman.

Every time.

Now, maybe X's father beat him

but in the last analysis, the responsibility for X is a woman's.

Women are responsible for children.

She should have calmed Mr. X down.

She should have called the police.

She should have been nicer to Mr. X so he wouldn't treat his children like that.

She should have left Mr. X.

If she did leave Mr. X, she should not have left him and deprived X of a father.

If she had a job, she was obviously neglecting X by not staying at home and mothering him.

If she did not have a job, she certainly should have been able to raise X to be happier than he was.

If she was rich, she obviously spoiled X.

If she was poor, she should have had more sense than to have had X.

If X was her only child, she failed X by not providing X with brothers and sisters.

If X had brothers and sisters, it is clear that she didn't give him enough attention.

If she was old, she had no business having X.

If she was young, she raised X badly because she didn't have enough experience.

If she was white and middle class, there is no excuse for her failure to provide X with the upbringing he needed (X's mass murder is amazing!)

If she was non-white, she had no business having X.

If she was black, she must have "dominated" X (between cleaning houses and barely keeping her family alive, as well as coping with her war-torn men)

If she was seen frequently with X, she was guilty of dominating X, no matter what her race.

If she was seen infrequently with X, she must have neglected X.

If she disciplined X, his raping a three year old girl and dumping her into an outdoor toilet is a rebellion against her.

If she did not, X turned out this way because she was lazy.

If she was dead, X never had a chance in life to be normal. (It's still her fault).

Women are responsible for children.

Women are responsible to protect them from everything, including the violence, indifference, ignorance or absence of Mr. X.

As Robin Morgan observed, women might not travel and have as much adventure as men, but they really move in psychology.

When men are present (if there are any), their behavior ranges from a low of outright abuse to a middling of indifference, to a real high if they are "good" fathers and play with the children for some measure of the extremely limited time both are awake and available to each other.

Even more rarely, men will do some token measure of the shitwork involved (cleaning up vomit; laundering clothes; changing diapers; washing butts; preparing food and cleaning it off the ceiling).

But those instances are rare because in the best of cases, when the man is truly willing to take an interest in the children during the trivial amount of time he is actually available to them or them to him, the woman may take care of all such "unimportant" work so that they can enjoy each other.

This does not escape the notice of children.

Children see who gets their hands greasy cooking dinner.

who sits and reads the paper; goes out into the street where the excitement is

who cleans the toilets, who does and does not tidy, who makes the beds

who is on the butt end of jokes

who is served and who does the serving; how often, and in what spirit.

Children can see very early and very clearly who is privileged and who is not.

Their lot is forcibly thrown in with that of the woman, but they know that *they do not want to be like her*.

They want to be privileged, too.

This has certain effects on boys and other effects on girls.

·⁂·

It's clear to children that only women "raise" children. No amount of propaganda to the contrary is ever going to blind them to this obvious fact entailed in the patriachal division of labor.

So boys know, early on, that that kind of work and all the shitwork entailed is reserved for women.

The boy's future is already unimpeded, in his mind. This conception of himself, of his future, already instills in him a confidence that the girl cannot enjoy.

The essence of the relationship between child and childworker is separation.

The little boy is wholly dependent on a woman. He awakens to discover that this person is different from himself.

He is dependent on an "other"!

He awakens ever further to discover that this person is a devalued shitworker who does not have the same privileges

as people like him.

It's a source of deep humiliation to all children that they have to be dependent on anybody. This is the cause of the most horrifying tantrums and frustrations of early life.

Little boys discover that not only are they dependent, but dependent on an "other"! And what is more, an *inferior* "other"!

That this person with whom they have a deep, nourishing emotional bond

is someone from whom they not only need to become separate (independent), but from whom they must differentiate themselves as much as possible, at all cost,

in order to esteem themselves:

in order to become what they really are,

remote and privileged men.

And as the full weight of gender crushes down on them as they approach the age of "reason" (You're not a baby anymore!) the pressure to become men creates an ever more agonizing situation for little boys, to rip themselves away from any identification with all of the things associated with women: from tenderness; from physical contact with her body; from emotion; from imitating nourishing behavior; from association with little girls (the future lower class, the "others")

from the childworker they desperately need and who is with them every day.

How can little boys do this?

Sandra Harding tells us,

they must dominate their feelings.

Moreover, in order to achieve the privileged status of the remote male, they have to also dominate others.

> Thus infant boys' psychological birth in families with our division of labor by gender produces men who will be excessively rationalistic, who will need to dominate not only others but also their feelings, their physical bodies, and other bodies—nature—in general. They will be excessively competitive and concerned primarily with their own projects. They will maintain an excessive separation or distance from the concerns of those around them, especially those unlike themselves. It produces misogyny and male-bonding as prototypes of appropriate social relations with others perceived to be respectively unlike and like themselves. (Harding, 152)

Devalued women go on being "responsible" throughout children's lives, regardless of race, economic class, or economic system.

Rich women pay poor women to fulfill "their" individual "responsibility." The childworker is still a devalued woman.

Nurseries and childcare centers are almost exclusively staffed by women.

In the United States, the government's 2000 census found that seventy-nine percent of all elementary and middle school teachers were women.

In the old Soviet Union, now Russia, Audre Lorde asked a woman named Madame Izbalkhan "whether 'men are encouraged to work in the kindergartens to give the children a gentle male figure at an early age.' Madame Izbalkhan hesitated for a moment. 'No,' she said, 'We like to believe that when the children come to the kindergarten they acquire a second mother'" (29).

As time goes on, whole organs of humanity are hacked off these emerging human beings: tenderness and affect, other relatedness from boys; self-confidence, self-assertion, intellect, physical strength and integrity, life/time from girls

as they are deformed to fit ever more firmly into the coffin molds of patriarchal social relations.

These gender roles (social relations) are reinforced (and only reinforced, not originated) by everything in children's lives, including television—how could little boys and girls possibly be exposed six hours a day to television images of women and not hold them in contempt?; differential teacher interactions and responses; language so loaded with exclusively male referents that it confers nonpersonhood on girls; restrictive, cold, fussy girls' clothing; active toys for boys and passive toys for girls; textbooks in which virtually all active and/or important humans are portrayed as males; loaded parental expectations; the outright exclusion of girls from many forms of sports; the witholding of meaningful sex education and contraceptives; the discouragement of young women from following "non-interruptible" careers; the mounting pressures on developing girls to nurture (forego life/time) their siblings, nurture their parents' needs, nurture their boyfriends; all-male history leaving girls isolated with no anchor in humanity; the inhibiting fear of abduction and sexual assault which imprison every temporal and spatial relation girls have with their environments,

just to mention a few patriarchal reinforcements in passing.

It takes an immense social machinery to reassure the patriarchal order that girls will be girls and boys will be boys. The basic production of this machinery and its operation are the labor of women. Once the product is achieved, the gendered individual, men take over its bitter 'profits.'

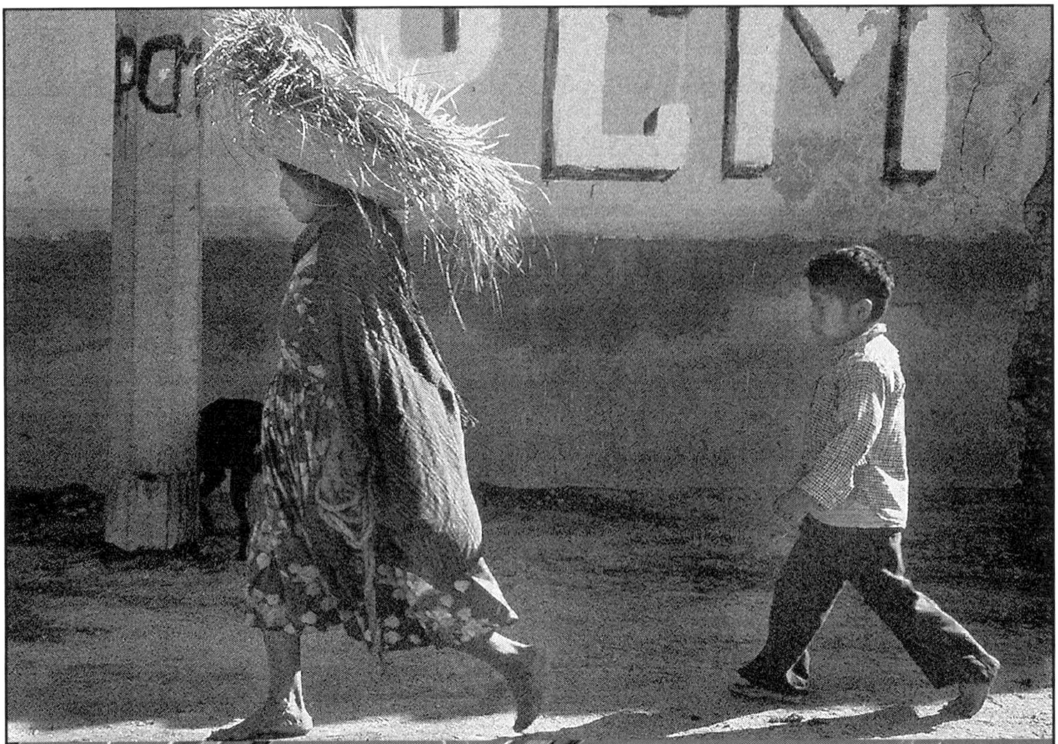

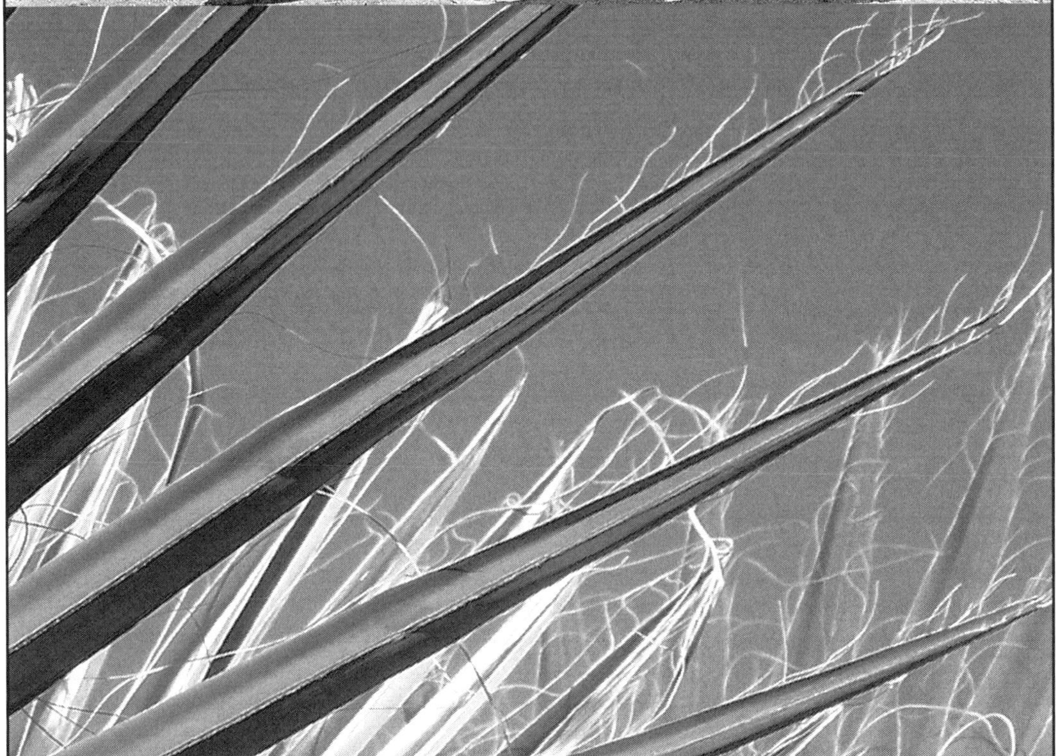

CHAPTER VI

Marxists and the Shortest Revolution

It is no greater irony that women are in charge of reproducing these social relations than it is that workers everywhere feed, clothe, and build the shelters of their oppressors.

It is no more mysterious than the connection between smoking and lung cancer, or the oppression of one economic class by another, and its solution is just as obvious, if difficult to achieve. The privileged gender of the social relations of reproduction has to be divested of its privileges and join the working class. That old axiom of socialism, "He who does not work, shall not eat" should have its counterpart in the relations of reproduction in some form:

>He who does not childwork shall not reproduce.

There's nothing mysterious in the social relations of reproduction, but they have been mystified by men who are ignorant and in whose interest it is to remain ignorant about those relations. "The longest revolution" is exactly what they wish women to believe it will be.

They hope it will be a long, long, long revolution.

They hope it will last forever, just so that it doesn't succeed.

Don't believe this weary stuff about "the longest revolution." It's the political equivalent of: "Baby, I've got really *important* things to do." (So you "stay" with the baby and peel the carrots).

It is the political equivalent of the religious promise of a real nice deal, after you die.

Don't be fooled by this "longest revolution" ploy, because it could be the shortest revolution on record. It wouldn't take more than one generation of human beings childworked by men and women equally to explode social relations into a whole new order of humanity.

It would not have to take very long at all and it is feasible to work on it right now, simultaneously with other progressive struggles.

·~·

Before going back and looking at that axiom "He who does not childwork shall not reproduce," which brings to mind all sorts of alarming ideas, I would like to consider Lenin.

Lenin espoused the ideas of Marx and Engels, and he understood that much of the misery of other humans was due to the existence of an economy which created "classes" of people. Of all the revolutionary males of those times, Lenin wrote most passionately against the subjugation of women.

In relation to women's oppression he said, "I want no part of the kind of Marxism which infers all phenomena and all changes in the ideological superstructure of society directly and blandly from its economic basis, *for things are not as simple as all that*" (Zetkin, 106) (emphasis mine).

He understood that something else was going on but he didn't understand patriarchy. He understood the oppression of workers as it stemmed from a capitalist division of labor, but didn't understand the oppression of women as it stemmed from a patriarchal division of labor.

In 1920 in the heat of efforts to preserve and consolidate the revolution he had helped guide, he asked a woman who was also a Marxist revolutionary, to help form an international revolutionary women's movement. He saw clearly that there could be no mass movement without women, and he asked Clara Zetkin to report on the work revolutionaries were doing among women.

Clara recorded the following conversation between herself and Lenin and it's worth remembering because it embodies all the contradictions that still divide feminists and Marxists—that still keep women out of revolutionary movements which their lives and futures as humans depend on, and which still keep men and women out of the gender revolution which their lives and futures as humans depend on. In fact, an effective mass revolutionary movement among women never got created, for reasons illuminated lucidly by this conversation.

Lenin and all the revolutionaries in Russia were staggering under the weight of the work it was taking to keep the revolution moving and propel it forward. There was no time for fooling around. Exasperated, he says to Clara, "I have been told that at the evenings arranged for reading and discussion with working women, sex and marriage problems come first. They are said to be the main objects of interest in your political instruction and educational work. I could not believe my ears when I heard that" (101).

Sex and marriage problems come first!

Here we are battling with the counter-revolutionaries of the whole world, and foremost in the minds of women are sex and marriage problems! Good grief.

How could this be?

Of course, we understand how this can be and still is. The great masses of women perceive their individual oppression and dehumanization as directly related to sex and marriage, with great accuracy. Most working women on the planet are not workers in what Marxists like to consider "basic industry." Their husbands, lovers, brothers, fathers and sons may be, but they are not. The only so-called "basic industry" women have ever been more than a minority in in industrial capitalist societies is the relatively recent one of electronics, which is a very important fact, because that industry is creating the means of production of the future, and because it is the most resistant of all industries to being unionized, largely because women are its workers. Efforts to organize it are still dominated by males and fashioned after the historical methods of organizing male dominated industries.

This doesn't mean women haven't been workers all along, of course. They work longer hours and harder than men in the far more basic industry of "reproduction," (in socializing the means of the means of production); in creating time for men; in servicing all human emotional needs outside of the social relations of "production"; in caring for the sick and aged; in producing all material goods and services necessary to human survival but not profitable,

as well as

being office workers, restaurant workers, seamstresses, maids, secretaries, teachers—service workers for the most part, workers in the lowest paid jobs—not high paid "basic industry" workers like autoworkers or transportation workers.

·⁂·

A "basic industry" as it is defined by Marxists is one which, if the workers in it go on strike, brings the whole economy to a halt. Organizing workers in basic industries is primary to an economic revolution because, the theory goes, by bringing the economy as it now exists to a grinding halt, workers can take power over the economy and make it serve their interests instead of the interests of a small class of rich people.

If all the transport workers in the United States went on strike, the economy would be paralyzed. If all the teachers went on strike, it would be annoying but the economy would go on.

Women who study revolutionary thought come upon this fact, sooner or later. And although it is never written or spoken about or formulated so to women, it becomes clear to women that if they are not workers in basic industry, (and the vast majority of them, outside of agricultural societies, are not), their role in the revolution, although it is "very important," is not crucial, except as it is "auxiliary" to the real revolution, which depends on men. Men are more important than women are in a Marxist analysis and there is no way around that fact.

·⊱⊰·

Many women have formed "auxiliary" organizations and supported union movements. They belong to the same economic class as men do even though they belong to a lower stratum of it. At times their work has been crucial. Women have made tremendous sacrifices to unionize their own secondary industries and thereby strengthened their economic class and bettered their lives and their families' lives.

They have done this with a clear sense of self-interest, as they understand themselves as economically oppressed, and understand that their men and children too are economically oppressed. Moreover they have frequently had to carry out this revolutionary activity in the face of screaming opposition not only of their husbands and significant male others but of male union officials and of workingclass men.

Women continue to do this.

But if you put them together in a room you will still find that what elicits the greatest interest and the most animated conversation among the great majority of women, whether they work in one of those secondary industries or not, is sex, marriage, and children.

This is not because women are trivial airheads.

It is because they are sex (emotional) workers, men (service) workers, and childworkers. Unlike men, they are not talking about matters unimportant to them. They are talking about their work.

Lenin should have believed his ears, not sent Clara Zetkin back to those meetings to inform the women that they were wrongheaded to "make" a priority out of their most deeply felt experiences. Change was in the air in the 1920s. Women sniffed in the air a chance for social changes that would liberate them as women, not only as workers in the economy that men acknowledged as real.

And they were told by Marxist revolutionaries that their priorities were all wrong. To fall into line and service the male-dominated revolution informed by a male worldview (theory), which depended for its success on male workers in basic industry. And their liberation would flow naturally, (albeit very, very slowly) from the revolutionary results.

Marxists are still telling this to women.

But women are still, notoriously, "backward."

Their backwardness is so great that many of them, for some time now have not been looking to Marxist revolutionaries for answers to their liberation, but have been organizing as women, in all sorts of unprecedented, spontaneous and bewildering ways. Political furor has erupted about abortion and child support and comparative wages and pornography and language and paternity leaves and (!) homosexuality and lesbianism and sex education and gender gaps and...

"It's all obviously a smokescreen to cover up the real revolution in basic industry," I was told by a communist once. (What's more it couldn't have any revolutionary validity because it crosses classes). Here, I am laughing at the Marxists, but not out of contempt.

For while there is a certain grim hilarity in expecting women to assume that patriarchy is on the way out when all women can cook for men on electric stoves, the Marxists have been committed, blood and bone, for a over a century, to creating an economic system in which everybody has enough food to cook in the first place.

⁂

Women and children are the vast majority of humans on this earth.

Women, children and men need each other, not only at an individual level, but at a political level. Marxists and feminists need each other. We need to amplify our vision of what revolution is and r(evolution) is not just about food.

⁂

It is strange to observe that Marxists have such a clear understanding of the fact that workers fight, and fight effectively, out of their own sense of oppression, not out of somebody else's version of their reality, and they can be so blind to what that means in terms of women. Women want a better economic life and what's more, do a disproportionate amount of the revolutionary shitwork just as they do in every other sphere of their lives. Many of them do it in an effort to make a better world for their children regardless of how it may affect them. Women are used to carrying other people's banners through one dimension or another, all of their lives. They are conditioned to sellf less behavior.

But this is qualitatively different, and will be quantitatively a whole other order of magnitude when women fight out of their own deeply felt personal sense of oppression as workers in the *whole economy of human survival*. Some form of socialism itself will be desirable to women, in fact will even be interesting to many women, when it includes concrete plans (and concrete priorities) for their freedom as women. This is a freedom which can only be achieved by changing the patriarchal division of labor in which women alone are responsible for childwork, a division of labor which results in the psychic amputation of men.

You can see, as time goes on, that the struggles of women to dismantle the social machinery that reinforces patriarchy forces men to concede a little here and concede a little there. Men will do all sorts of fancy footwork accommodating this bit of language usage, that token position. Eventually, they will be forced to open all the positions in the male hierarchy of power to women. It will cost us superhuman struggles, but it will be achieved. Patriarchy can afford to do this without risking substantial loss of male privilege, because as long as the great masses of women are exhausted by the patriarchal division of labor,

as long as the life/*times* of women are constantly consumed by all the extra labor they do, there will never be a chance that the great masses of them will ever be empowered to take full advantage of those "opportunities."

⋄

This doesn't mean that changing language usage or fighting for "male" jobs or fighting for better wages are trivial struggles, as every gain made in those domains empowers women. It means that those struggles need to be informed by the intent to overthrow patriarchy at its *base*, and its base is the exclusive responsibility of women for childwork.

⋄

Years ago on the radio I heard William Mandel interview a Soviet woman scientist who ran a research institute employing over a hundred people. It wasn't common, even in the Soviet Union, for a woman to be at the head of a research institute that size, so she was a symbol of what women could achieve under the Soviet version of socialism. She freely admitted that, as a manager, she did not like to hire women because the women got pregnant and in the socialist system she had to give them up to a year's leave of absence while keeping their jobs for them and it was very inconvenient to do that, it hurt the research. She was a manager in a system claiming to be better than the capitalist system, among many other reasons because she could do a "male" job in it. And she was doing a good male job of it.

·⁓⁓·

As long as childwork is exclusive to women, women can only fully avail themselves of such "opportunities" if they are willing to forego having children at all, which is unacceptable; or if they are willing to relinquish the greatest and most rewarding part of childwork to other women, which is also unacceptable.

This latter "choice" is unacceptable because of the desire of women to participate meaningfully in the development of the children they took the trouble to have.

Relinquishing the greatest and most rewarding part of childwork to other women, in exchange for being able to fully avail themselves of job "opportunities" is also absolutely unacceptable, because as long as childwork is performed exclusively by women, children will continue to be gendered just as they are now. Patriarchy will continue to be reproduced in little girls and little boys, no matter how many reforms we make in its reinforcements.

·⁓⁓·

Most women in the United States are poor. In fact, the "feminization of poverty" is baldly making an economic class out of our gender class. Even women who live well are poor because the majority of them are not owners of the wealth they enjoy nor do they have the power to sustain it. They are dependent, with relatively few exceptions, on men, either in the context of private patriarchy or of public patriarchy. And yet, even though they have no objective interest in capitalism, even though these millions of poor women have no firm economic stake in this system, they balk at socialism.

Political propaganda targeted at women which is most effective is aimed at their imperatives as workers in the patriarchal system. They're told that under any system other than the prevailing one, power over their children will be taken away from them. That their churches (the only source of solace or community for millions of women) will be taken away from them; that the shitwork they already do will be immeasurably expanded by lack of consumer goods; that they will have no freedoms and there will be no joy, color, warmth, or spontaneity in life.

There you are. No power over their children. No power over their religion. Fat/starving, overworked, oppressed, uptight. In reality, this describes the conditions of most women under advanced capitalism.

There are many lies in the propaganda barrage targeted at women, but the most powerful is the one about losing power over their children. It manipulates the fears women have of being separated; of their children being ghettoized away from them at an early age; of losing the rewards of meaningful participation in their children's lives, and of their children losing the rewards they have to offer them. It is confidence in themselves and in the (real!) rewards there are that lead women who have any choice in the matter to have children in the first place. Women simply do not see themselves as cattle breeding children for the good and welfare of the state, any state.

Not only are the rewards of childwork real, but they are the only deeply meaningful ones life has to offer many women in the system we live in. (Also true is that the one-to-one interchanges with a loving childworker with a shared personal history are some of the deepest and most positive experiences of childhood).

Women in the U.S. are suspicious of what a socialist order would mean to them as childworkers, and resent propaganda which portrays them as backward and uneducated because they are not so enlightened as to desire the exclusion of their children from their working lives.

·⸛·

In reality, all women and all children would be far better off in a system socialized such that there are good nurseries, kindergartens, and healthcare provided by a state. While it isn't ideal, a kindergarten supervised by women where children are safe, decently fed, and can interact with one another, is vastly better than no kindergarten at all. In such a system, children are guaranteed both preventative and curative health care, education, and a future with a possible job in it. Women would have more power over their own and their children's lives because they would not be so economically dependent on men. Legal patriarchy can be abolished, so that they are liberated from the (legal) struggles for abortion rights, divorce rights, pensions and education.

I think that some socialist order is a prerequisite for the liberation of women, but it doesn't guarantee liberation from patriarchy. It isn't enough to facilitate women's double load. Women liberated to do "men's" work through the employment of other women to do childwork full time is just a more efficient form of patriarchy.

In Cuba, where some meaningful advances in human welfare have been made by socialism, the government even tried to codify some laws to ease the double load. In a document called *Sobre El Pleno Ejercicio de la Igualdad de la Mujer: Tesis y Resolución*, concerns about liberating women focused on how to facilitate shopping for working women (not on men's sharing the task): "To study the business hours of commercial enterprises in order to establish, throughout the country, those which best fit the needs of working women" (143). There were also concerns about how to establish part-time working schedules so that women (not men) still without childcare facilities could take care of children without giving up other work entirely; on organizing special education courses at hours that childworking women (not men) could attend; on how to "increase, in work centers with appropriate conditions, nurseries for the children of working mothers" (144), not on how to "increase, in work centers with appropriate conditions, nurseries for the children of working fathers."

Although formally men were charged with "equal" responsibility both for childwork and housekeeping and although the document explicitly stated that "The concept that child care is the exclusive province of the mother should be rejected," in fact, the document assumes, realistically, that it is women who are doing both the childwork and the housework.

The parasitism of men expressed in this assumption is lamented as an expression of old, out-dated bourgeois "attitudes" which must change.

One has to be grateful to the Cuban women who pushed things to the point at which a state even recognized and what is more concerned itself with the time and effort women are forced to invest in childwork, shopping, and housework. But it is inescapable that it is women who do these things.

It isn't "attitudes" that can change this state of affairs. The "attitudes" are not based on some withering vestige of the old order, do not come prepackaged out of history into the minds of newborns, but are based on observations of the everyday reality of the patriarchal division of labor which all children make. These are of a system in which all humans are initiated into all of the pains, contradictions, possibilities and limitations of human life itself through a fiercely intimate complex of prerational experiences and associations dominated exclusively by women. This powerful complex of feelings underlies and resonates along the entire continuum of human development and into death.

(I still remember the recorded words of the PSA pilot over San Diego in 1980, on the radio, whose plane had collided with a smaller aircraft and who plunged to his death saying "I love you, mother.")

(And the mass murderer who gunned down twenty-one people, most of them children—and most of them non-white, "other,"—in San Diego in 1984, growling as he entered the restaurant, "Get out of my way, you mothers!").

Men who consider themselves progressive complain that gender "attitudes" are not "rational" and they're right. They are deeply rooted in female-dominated prerational experience.

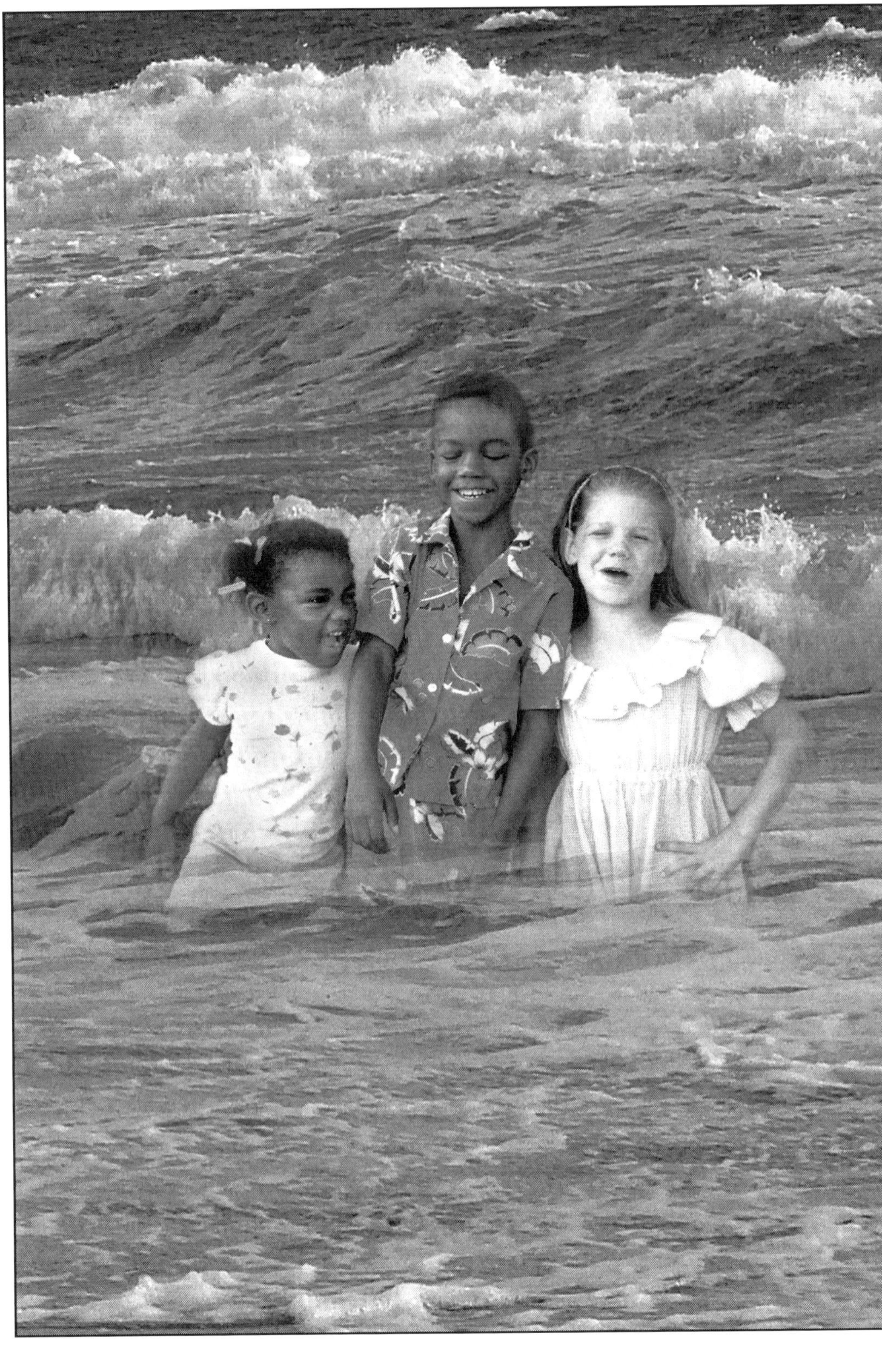

CHAPTER VII

Color: The Dispersion of Light

Racism in this country of our birth is the hardest to write about because I'm white. But because I am, it's my responsibility to tread over this minefield with you. It isn't the responsibility of non-white people to teach you the bloody history of your white ancestors or the meaning of the skin privilege you have inherited and continues to be maintained by forms of violence today.

People of color resent it when white women compare their oppression to racism and white women would do well to leave such comparisons to the only people qualified to make them, which is to say, women of color. All oppressions have in common the dehumanization of the oppressed and they all oppress in some ways which are similar but experienced (and therefore only fully knowable, in depth and scope) by the humans being dehumanized.

Racism and sexism are engendered by our whole economic system, but have different histories. While the origins of patriarchy can reasonably be said to have originated in physical difference which had real economic significance, skin color has no economic significance whatsoever. Racism is special form of cruelty even by the nature of its absurdity as a measure of difference in the first place.

Racism against blacks grew here out of slavery, but it is extended to all people of color. Slavery existed because it was very profitable to a relatively small class of people. Humans of different colors have practiced or been victims of slavery—it is not dependent on a particular color, but on an economic system which made it a (possible) and profitable institution. (Today, blacks still enslave blacks in the chaotic economy of Sudan). I mention this because you must never hate your own flesh. We are not racists because we are white.

There is a great danger in "white" guilt. If we feel guilty because we are white, we are feeling guilty about something over which we have no control. This eliminates the responsibility to do anything about our racism.

As long as we continue (inside and outside of ourselves) to educate ourselves about racism; as long as we steadfastly fight it (in both places) we need feel no guilt. If we ignore it, we are guilty of ignore (ance) (racism): of the abuse of millions of women, children, and men.

Racism is profitable for the same reason slavery was profitable to landowners in the early days of our country: it provides cheap labor to run industries and work the land, so that a small group of people can get more profits. The profits of racism grow out of the divisions it creates among people: as long as people can be kept divided, they can't organize (unionize) themselves and get a larger share of the wealth they produce.

Note that even though we work hard and produce wealth (and take wealth from other countries so that we are one of the richest countries in the world), we can't even be assured of health care; we can't be sure of our jobs; we are poorly educated; we may (especially those of us who are women) die in poverty even if we worked hard all our lives; many people don't even have housing or enough food. Capitalists insist that healthcare must be a profit-making "industry," that all human housing must provide them profits, that we be discarded once we are no longer instrumental in producing profits for them.

That small capitalist class of people spends the wealth we make on themselves, on bombs and on building bureaucracies and military machines to expand and maintain their power. That small (really very vulnerable) capitalist class of people has a nightmare, which is that the people whom they exploit for their profits might get organized and kick them out of their plush offices and run the economy in a way which is in the interest of the majority of humankind.

As long as people are nice and divided, it won't ever happen. The greatest capitalist power in the world is the United States, and it is the capitalists in the U.S. who have the most to lose from the dreaded spectre of racial unity.

Within the U.S., this means that the majority (white people who are not capitalists) must be kept ignorant (racist) or keep ourselves ignorant (racist) toward people of color so that we can't work together in the interest of the economic class we both belong to.

The majority in the United States (white people who are not capitalists) must also be kept ignorant of or keep ourselves ignorant of people of color in order for white people to overlook what the capitalist class of the U.S. is doing to people of color outside of the U.S. (most of the world), which is even less cosmetic than what they are doing within it.

Since racism is only in the economic interest of a small group of people, it would be logical to assume that it is just this small group of people (the capitalist class), who are responsible for racism.

But that's not the way it works. In this country, racism grew first out of slavery. Slavery, as it evolved in the United States, was based on *white* supremacy. *All* the whites had to be able to dominate all blacks at some level, because it could not have been enforced any other way. If just certain whites had supremacy, other whites could have indifferently ignored slaves escaping or slaves fighting back. The slaves could even have made friends with other whites. The system would have collapsed.

Slavery was so hideous that it could not even be witnessed by white people without some justification, much less be carried out. Not all white people could afford slaves. It was so bloody, violent, and repugnant, such a brutal violation of the humanity of its perpetrators as well as its enslaved victims', that an ideology had to be formed around it in order for the self esteem of the slaveowners and, no less important, the self-esteem of the whites who were not slaveowners, to be kept intact.

Self esteem is as necessary to human survival as food.

The importance of protecting their (highly valued) selves from what they were doing (or allowing to be done by not interfering with it), is well documented in the history of slavery and continues to be documented in the recorded thought of white people right now.

At that time (and this is still going on; it still has currency as a defense of racism), we told ourselves that we had to save them for God. They were savages and heathens whose souls needed processing to be acceptable to God. God needed us to do this work. It was our burden. He had charged us with the spiritual emancipation of all these ungrateful, uncivilized creatures. We tried to explain the benefits of hard work and the humble acceptance of God's will into their lives, but they were so intransigent about their heathen ideas that we were compelled to use force in defense of the will of God, in order to give them their spiritual freedom.

"By far the least costly way to preserve freedom is to build and maintain an adequate defense." (Lockheed Corporation)

People of color (and especially black people) had to be perceived as subhuman and they had to be perceived as subhuman by all white people, not just slaveowners.

Capitalism itself, as we know it and live in it, was made possible by the wealth created by slaves and all white people have benefited from capitalism in the measure that capitalism represents an advance over the systems which preceded it. Even in this context we have made the progress we have at the expense of people of color, who have never shared even near equally with whites the benefits of the system they made possible.

Economically, all whites had to have a stake in slavery and economically slavery afforded them the hope of buying a slave or two of their own, to relieve them of at least some of the shitwork to fulfill *their* economic needs, so that even whites who were living at a very marginal scale compared to the big landowners were provided with benefits or at the very least, *hope* that they could achieve benefits.

But these economic benefits were not all. At an individual level, where it could be felt by all whites no matter how miserable, what the great majority of poor white people got out of it (and this is stomach-churning) was self-esteem. Racism gave them some people to compare themselves to. It gave them people to measure themselves *in relation to* who made them look powerful. Made it look like they weren't so bad off. Because no matter how bad off they were under the brutal social and economic conditions prevailing in those times, they were better off than slaves.

Racism "told" them that the economic system they lived in was in their interest. It is still informing white people that they are progressing, by giving them this highly visible group of people to progress in relation to, in much the same way that the visible (apparently unmoving) mass of a mountain "informs" us that we are moving.

People of color are not only forced to labor at the dirtiest, most unrewarding labor required by our visible economic system (and the fruits of this labor are measurable, at least theoretically, in numbers of dollars accumulated by the capitalist class), but are forced to produce self esteem for all white people as well. They do this by suffering. They have to suffer worse than we do. That is their job, in what might be called the racist division of labor. This work consumes enormous amounts of time and energy not measurable in dollars, but which accumulates to the self image of all whites. The spectacle of human misery provided by racism provides a background against which to *feel* fortunate, and feeling fortunate is a very good feeling indeed. Racism makes us *feel good*. For no matter how "bad" we feel that those people live in such terrible conditions, we're sure lucky *we* don't have to live like that or have those problems. Those problems aren't *ours*.

Whew!

Thank God.

We might be having a lot of problems at work, but at least we have a job. And there's a lot of problems in the world, what with wars and bad government and potholes in the highways, but things could be worse.

Given the objective reasons for racism, what this means is that we have enslaved ourselves with our own ignorance.

Overcoming that ignorance is not an easy thing to do because what we are negotiating in this part of the economy of racism is our self esteem, and self esteem is as important to humans as food. Its roots are down in the most vulnerable, desperately defended source of human need.

We mask—even from ourselves—our ignorance with all the resources and the strength we have to defend our selves.

At one level there are whites whose ignorance is masked by a real belief that people of color are subhuman. Their mommies and daddies told them so and their whole lives have been built on that premise, one thoroughly reinforced by their culture. These whites have eyes. But they choose to be offended by the very existence of people of color. These whites "know" that people of color live in those terrible conditions because they are lazy, ignorant, prone to crime, and "animal-like." And the reason they are is that they are born that way. This is not the responsibility of white people.

These whites are blatantly racist. Racism makes them feel good, feel superior. They defend their human superiority (their ignorance) by actively persecuting people of color any time that superiority is defied and sometimes just for the good, "superior" feeling provided by lashing out at corruption, poverty, crime and bestiality, which people of color conveniently embody for them. They do this by blowing up black churches, lynching young men, raping and terrorizing women and children, shooting at Mexicans as they come across the border—and in general abusing and humiliating people of color every chance they get. These white people are very blatant about their racism (ignorance), which operates on a scale ranging from smirks to murder.

Further along the ignorance continuum (but not much further) are the more sophisticated masks elaborated by educated ignorant whites. Their racism assures them that those people of color live under those terrible conditions because they are:

"Unfortunate." (They had the bad luck to be born with dark skin. This is not the responsibility of white people.)

"Underdeveloped." (They need to "catch up" with us. Not our responsibility.)

"Underprivileged." (They haven't earned the privileges we enjoy. They only need to work a little longer or a little harder. Not our responsibility.)

"Disadvantaged." (Their skin is a calamity. Not our responsibility.)

In other words, people of color are lazy (underprivileged), ignorant (disadvantaged), prone to crime and animal-like (underdeveloped), but it isn't because they were born that way.

It's because they live under those terrrible conditions. They would be fully human and civilized if they didn't have to live under those awful conditions created by racists (other white people). Racism is the responsibility of *other* white people.

This form of racism not only assures whites that people of color are subhuman (masks their ignorance), but it assures them that they are not racists because they do not bomb churches or use the word "nigger," and this increases their self-esteem very much, not only by giving them, in addition to people of color, a whole group of *white* people to feel superior to, but by giving them numberless opportunities to display their superiority to those other white people by being "nice" to people of color. When a person of color gives a speech or shares a social event, after that person is gone, these white people outdo each other describing that person of color as intelligent, refined, articulate, well-dressed, (even good-looking!) as if that were an amazing fact or at least quite remarkable, and bask together in the glow of the self esteem that comes from knowing that one is not a racist: is not responsible for racism.

Yet further along the ignorance continuum (for it continues), are the masks devised by radical whites. The racism of those whites assures them that people of color live under those terrible conditions because they are exploited, disenfranchised, and abused by the capitalist class (other whites).

Our racism assumes that since people of color are human (not apes) they are just like us! And this provides us with a measure of self esteem incomparably greater than that felt by other whites, not only because it gives us superiority over *all* other whites, but because it allows us to see ourselves as the liberators of the world (which is mostly made up of people of color). We're not just "nice." We're heroic!

We do not "liberate" people of color by killing them

Nor do we "liberate" people of color by donating money to help them form themselves in our image,

We "liberate" them by showing them that they are like us!

All they have to do to find this out is to join one of our organizations.

We know that we are not racist because we are willing to work with them as equals. On our terms, of course. Our terms are that they treat *us* as equals, not as if we were racists. Not as if we were ignorant. If they do not find this convincing (and they do not find this convincing), we have class analysis to prove that we are equal. We are all workers of the world. Of course, they have suffered worse than we have. (This has been their job all along). But this is behind us now. We've found each other and we can work against the common enemy, capitalism. And we will pay real special attention to them because we know that the real difference between us is that they have suffered more than we have. (Suffering worse than we do is their job, isn't it? That's what defines them, isn't it?)

We will do this by fighting all (those other) white racists. And if people of color are still not convinced (and they still are not convinced), we will display our suffering credentials to show them how much like us they really are. We are women and know what oppression is. We are workers and know what oppression is. We are Catholics and know what oppression is. We are Jews and know what oppression is. We are all one in our suffering. It's amazing how hard it is for them to understand this, but we try to be patient.

But they are not convinced. Their intransigent ideas about us being racist are just downright ignorant. Ungrateful, too. In addition to this, they create a lot of division dragging racism up all the time. Prone to crime of this sort against the revolution. Uneducated in the finer points of revolution.

This equation of people of color with suffering denies their humanity. As if all they ever did was suffer. As if that's who they are. As if who they are is defined by their relations to us. This perception of them is subhuman. There you have it. Subhuman, ungrateful, ignorant, uneducated, prone to crime...

This view has always been most important to us, to make us feel good; feel fortunate; feel titillated; feel the satisfaction of giving them some charity; feel above their suffering, which is to say, above them. So when we haul out our suffering credentials and display them in an effort to prove to people of color that they are like us, it is just about one of the most racist and insulting damn displays of our ignorance that there is.

People of color are not like us. The ways in which they are not like us are that they are not as privileged as we are and they are not as ignorant as we are. They are not as ignorant about themselves, and they are not as ignorant about us. They do not want to be like us. They want to share justly in the wealth they produce so that they will not be poor, but there is a huge difference between wanting not to be poor, and wanting to be like us.

It is a measure of the ignorance expressed in an exclusively Marxist analysis of the human economy that material goods are what it's all about; that the attainment of material security defines human happiness. Most people of color have not been on the receiving end of many of the material benefits of capitalism. They haven't necessarily formed their culture around money, or isolated themselves from each other in the ways we have isolated ourselves from each other. They have developed relations and knowledge in cultural dimensions of their own.

I want to be very careful here, around this particular mine. There is a racism mine here which, when it explodes, sends up a big white banner that reads "Oh, they have suffered and their suffering has made them beautiful and spiritual." (Therefore we have done them a favor). It is not more beautiful to have a mouth full of rotten teeth because you can't afford a dentist than it is to have a mouth full of well-cared-for teeth. Suffering is definitely not beautiful.

There are some white people who sense that somehow those people have knowledge which we do not have which makes their cultures and those people themselves, very attractive. If you ever strip enough racism off yourself to compare your culture with theirs, it comes up as shriveled in some ways by comparison.

So you disown your culture.

Now, this is a very painful position to be in.

Here you are with a racist family, having gone to racist schools, lived in white neighborhoods, listened to white music, filled your head with white literature, and all your friends are white and racist to some degree or another. What can you do?

Some white people try to "assimilate" into the cultures of people of color and this takes some very pathetic forms like people who grab a solidarity movement and try to live and breathe only some other culture.

Here I step around another mine. It takes courage to be white and stand truly in solidarity with people of color and it is not some game, but an obligation. They need white people who will be listened to by whites and this is one of the concrete things we can do to serve both people of color and ourselves.

What I want to point out is that this obligation needs to be fulfilled as a white person, not as an ersatz colored person. We can't disown our families even if they disown us. We can't abandon our own people into the morass of ignorance we have clambered a few levels out of, and throw ourselves into the laps of people of color as though they could save us from our racism.

What our white culture has done is not simply separate us from people of color; it has separated us from each other. We only separate ourselves further from one another by running and hiding behind people of color. White people are not fooled by this. They know who we are. Nor do we have credibility as "colored" among people of color. It elicits contempt, although they usually strain to be polite about it. We have to work things out among ourselves.

I'm not of the school of breastbeating whites who disown us; who see us as damned forever by our past; who romanticize people of color as our saviors who are going to come and cut our ugly heads off and so save the world. They really have better things to do. Have you ever killed a snail? Anything bigger than a snail? I had to shoot a cow once and I've never gotten over it.

I say this with confidence: the vast majority of people of color don't want to kill us. The most powerful movement ever organized and executed against white power in this country was informed by the vision of Dr. Martin Luther King, Jr., and his vision was one of harmony among races, of black children and white children together. There is no "Kill the honky" rhetoric which burns up out of the rage of a people raped which has ever so moved the masses of people of color. Of course, that doesn't mean that "Kill the honky" is not possible. Dr. King himself said "Those who make peaceful revolution impossible make violent revolution inevitable."

I am just saying that's not what they want to do.

It isn't necessary to put people of color in the awful position of having to mercy kill us. We do have something to offer. I look at you, at your unfolding beauty, at you and a black toddler rubbing each other's hair and shrieking in *delight* at the difference. I look inside myself and see my mischievous beauty, my subversive beauty sneaking around my attempts to act straight;

I look at my racist uncles and don't just see ignorance. I see three wiry men who were orphaned in a world at war, who set their pug Irish noses straight ahead and wrested a living out of the brutal waterfronts of the world, setting out to sea at thirteen, fourteen, fifteen years of age. Little boys who had never learned to swim; who have spent their whole lives at sea and still can't swim. I know my uncles are human because they have the unbelievable gall to sit around and ask me why it took me so long to learn to drive.

My uncles are so outrageous one of them got off a ship, spent six months wages taking a taxi round trip from port to Idaho to visit us and got back on the ship for another round, dead broke.

One of them saved me from myself; saved all of the rest of my life for me.

Another one of them got off a ship he had been gone on so long he didn't even know I lived in that port, bumped into me in the street during a demonstration he didn't understand and which I didn't understand at the time, either. It was against the SACB, the Senate version of the House UnAmerican Activities Committee. What I knew was the guy they had hauled in there was a man who lived in a house with a student wife surrounded by six kids and the necessity to childwork them all and ran a seamen's soupline on the side. And I did deeply feel that any man who could wipe six asses with that kind of aclarity and run a soupline on the side might be UnAmerican but certainly wasn't a threat to humanity.

Well anyway this uncle walked right around the federal building with me, all natty like my uncles always are, those men dress nice and they held their five foot three own in the male pecking order from Kowloon to Anchorage and even their frequently broken noses are kind of jaunty and he kept walking right around the federal building with me, past the clutch of costumed Daughters of the American Revolution shrieking at us from the corner and past the police barricades and said he didn't see much in this demonstrating and all but how was I doing in school and so on, politely accompanying me, round and round the federal building and the feds and the police motorcycles and the barricades in that tumultuous demonstration, carrying on a visit with me with his impeccable sense of family propriety and he took me out to a nice restaurant afterwards.

And another of them, the youngest, who had learned early like all of them that marijuana didn't turn you into a fiend, was a man I could turn on with and stare at the lazy circles in the lake and hear the fat birds land on the little houseboat he had saved enough to buy and rowed out to when he was in port because he was a man who loved the water, even if he never learned how to swim.

These uncles of mine were blatant racists. Their sense of self-esteem was so fragile; they were so ignorant of their own beauty, that they tried to make themselves look good by badmouthing people who don't look like them. And what's more, they did this on purpose, from time to time, in a kind of bantam rooster male solidarity display, their red hair flaming like combs on their heads, around me. Especially for my benefit. My uncles not only thought they were harmless doing this, they thought they were cute. And I was forced to see

    these men I need to love

    these men whose love I always ached for

as stupid and vicious.

This is where the revolution, the only revolution we can truly claim our own, awaits us. It is all exciting to get a ticket to foreign struggles and stand on the borders thumbing our noses at Uncle Sam,

but uncle Larry

in the decidedly unexotic territory of the living room

is the critical expedition.

·⁂·

I look beyond our corporate capitalist culture and see that there is a human culture there, trying to be born. Its poems and its literature struggle to survive on debt-loaded presses and now surge onto the Net. John Brown lived. There were white women who fought slavery and lynching. There were whites who followed the movement of Dr. Martin Luther King into the south even though some of them were tortured to death in the swamps of Mississippi. There were whites on the picketlines in Oakland supporting the longshoremen who refused to unload South African ships. We have been human all along and the best of our humanity emerges. It just doesn't emerge enough.

We are agents of this emerging culture. You don't need to be afraid of your ignorance. When you discover a piece of it, pick it up like you would pick up any other piece of garbage you produce, and put it in a garbage can. And go right on ahead and fly your long straight shiny brown hair like a flag. Don't berate whites for their racism all stiff and righteous. They are already paralyzed with fear. Address them as someone still ignorant yourself. Show them they don't have to be afraid. Just go right on and flaunt that unintimidated outwhitelaw beauty of yours.

Inspire other whites to want to be like you.

If the fight against racism is, as it is interpreted to be by so many of our people, self-flagellation, disowning of the self, white people will never join it. They can't.

·⁂·

Now I am going to detonate this mine.

People of color are racist. They are racist toward one another. They call each other nigger, spic, chink, beaner. They can be found to discriminate in favor of their lighter members. Some of them do this within their immediate families. You hear black people disdain Vietnamese. See Mexican people huff up in contempt at the mention of blacks. Blacks disparge browns.

Amid the carnage you can discern black and brown children beating each other into unconsciousness, brown women spurning brown men in favor of white men; black men spurning black women in favor of white women; little girls straightening their black sea flowering hair in self hatred.

> This looks like a place we whites can get some peace
>
> knowing that they do it too
>
> It isn't just us.
>
> What a relief.
>
> Because if they are doing it, too, it isn't our fault.
>
> It's obviously human nature.
>
> We all know that it will take a very, very long time to change human nature, if it can ever be changed at all. Human nature is not our responsibility.

·☙❧·

Racism isn't based on color, but on power, a relationship between powerful and powerless. In this country, it is white people who have power. None of the discrimination practiced by people of color in relation to one another serves to give them any power. It serves only to enforce white power and it originates, in these circumstances, in white power.

Given the distribution of power in the hands of white racists, that long shudder of racism which emanates from whites, that wave of negative energy blasts through the bodies and minds of all humans subjected to it all through the color spectrum of humanity seeking its prime target, the beautiful blue glancing interstellar black of the bodies of Africans, and is forcibly internalized like the shredded tissue left behind by a bullet.

Everyone needs to feel self-esteem in this grotesque system that has come to be associated with feeling that one is progressing in relation to someone else. But not just anybody else. Somebody darker.

It takes an enormous amount of economic, legal, police, and military power to enforce this white racism which makes such behavior appear to be in anybody's interest in the first place.

•⊰⊱•

   Here's a warning and a better path: Don't jump at any hostility or distrust you may experience with people of color. It's a reaction to racism. It is based on long, objective experience with white people. This does not mean you have to take any shit from anybody, it just means that you have to recognize distrust for what it is and not get baited back into the racist battlefield.

In practice, the real hostility, the hand to hand, eye to eye combat you are going to be forced into in your efforts not to be a racist is going to come from other whites. In practice, it is not really any of these nutzo arguments that enforce racism among whites. Those arguments only mask the exercise of white power. And when you try not to be a racist, when you try to eliminate racism,

that power will be exercised against you.

This operates on a continuum beginning in your own home.

"She is my mother. I don't want to hurt her by pointing out that what she just said was racist. She has suffered enough. Anyway she is never going to change..."

"He is my husband. Things are hard enough between us as it is. I don't want to risk my whole marriage showing him how racist he is..."

"This is my child. The neighborhood women keep finding reasons why their children can't visit her here since so many Black and Spanish-speaking people come through the house..."

"This is my father-in-law. If I prohibit racist talk when he comes to visit, he'll never help us with a down payment on a house...""

"This is my friend. I don't want to alienate her..."

Even in well-meaning organizations, you will see the ritual dance of white racist solidarity jerk whole groups of people into the unconscious formation of a solid white wall and so enforce white power over the meeting, and white leadership of the group.

•⊰⊱•

You will not experience that white racist power in the same way that people of color experience it, because you will always have the option to shut up, toe the white line, and have your white privileges restored. But if you choose to fight racism, white people can and will isolate you from (even family) affection and esteem; from jobs; from upward mobility in jobs, and will discourage you from membership in their organizations.

And when the fight gets tough and open,

whites will jail you, too;
shoot you, too.

It is not the hostility of people of color that you have to worry about defending yourself from, it's white power.

Learning to recognize racism is the first step toward overcoming it, but once you recognize it, what can you do about it? Simply calling whites on their racism will keep you tangled up in interminable nutzo argument skirmishes on racist turf. Often you have to do this. Confronted with direct racism attacks, you have to do this, but over the long run, if you want to win, you have to devise strategies to kill their racism on territory remote from their defenses; and you have to do this in a minority position in white territory.

In other words, you have to engage in a kind of loving guerilla warfare.

And I say loving, because we cannot disown our families, our friends, our comrades or coworkers. Loving because, for whites, the first objective in the fight against racism is to get white people together against it: to end the divisions which racism enforces among us.

There are no blueprints for guerilla warfare, but there are some general directions. It is essential to respond when people of color ask us to participate in political struggle with them, whether it is a march against immigration authorities; a celebration of Dr. Martin Luther King Jr.'s birthday; a teach-in; a demonstration. This is essential. It shows that we desire to eliminate racism, but it does not eliminate it because most racism is unconscious.

To eliminate it, we have to learn about people of color, not just about racism. This means actively engaging in acquiring knowledge from people of color, regularly. The direction is not from them to us, but from us to them. This requires that we initiate the journey. This requires effort. Movement.

The first general direction is to stop ignoring them. Listen to them. Find out who they are from them, not from white TV, white sociologists, white anecdotes, but from them. One of the easiest and most rewarding ways to do this is to read what they write. Is your reading lily white, asks Alice Walker. If it is, it is racist. Seek out and attend public forums where they speak. Seek out and attend any cultural event they wish the public to attend. Subscribe to and read periodicals they control....Color your mind.

Do this learning unobtrusively, on their terms. Don't get up and ask them to talk about racism. It's they you want and need to learn about. Racism you learn about from observing white people from the perspective you will gain by paying attention to people of color.

This learning will explode a lot of information at you, not just about racism, but a whole perspective on human life and human relations, on everything humans ever think about and feel, because racism is not the only thing in this world they have any knowledge about. They have an immense body of information, analysis, understanding, experience, wonder, and electric joy to share with the white minority.

Armed with this growing perspective, you can begin to engage in loving guerilla warfare, smuggling more and more ammunition (information) from people of color into white racist territory, to ambush white racism with.

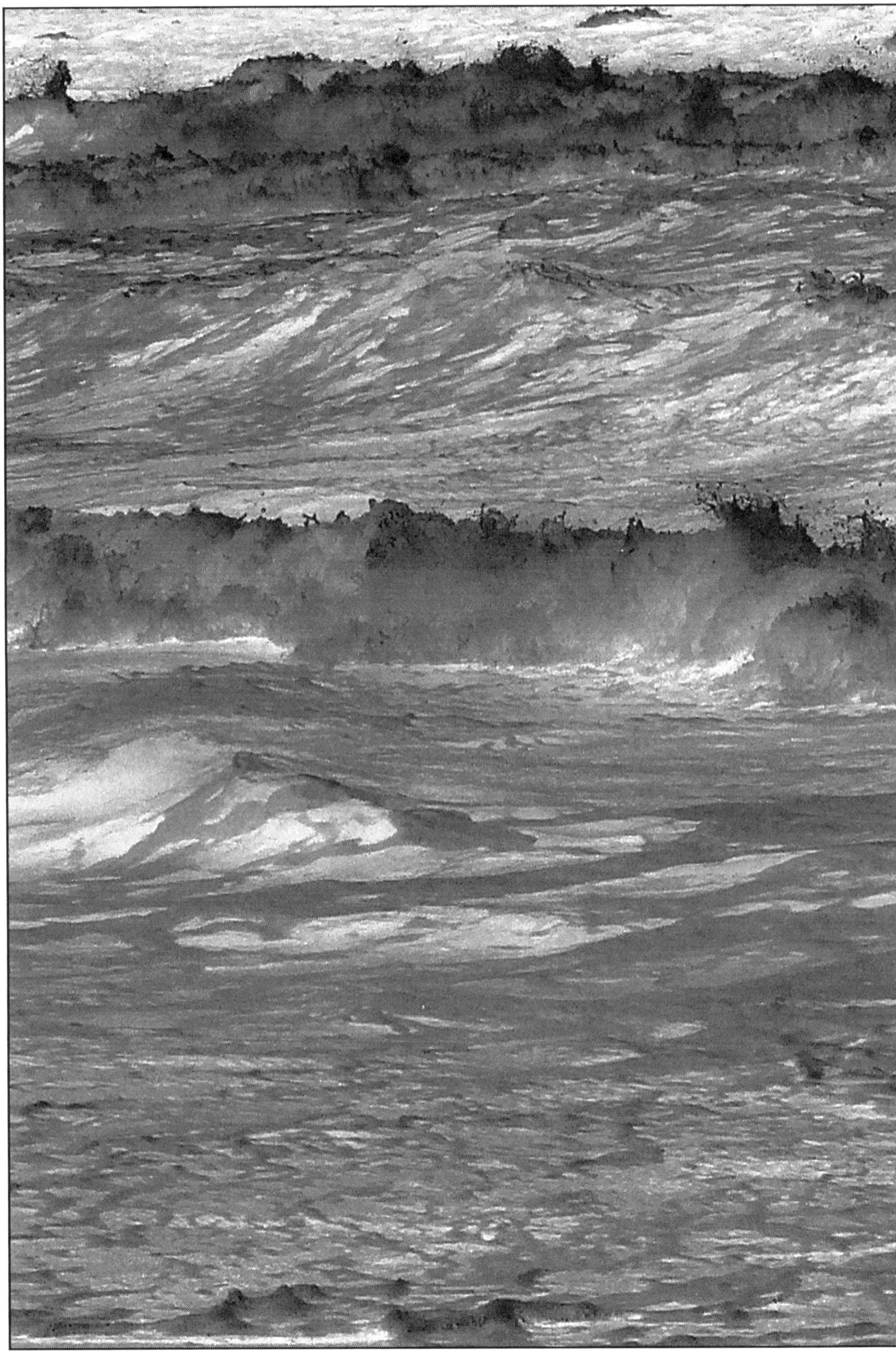

CHAPTER VIII

Patriarchy and Racism: Propagating Waves

If two waves have definite phases, they can add up in phase to provide a disturbance of twice the amplitude. But if coherent waves are brought together in such a way that their phases are opposite, they interfere destructively with one another. In the case of light waves, this means that light added to light can produce the absence of light—total darkness. (*Physical Science Today*)

"An eclipse!" (Zakiyah Ansari)

·⋙⋘·

In the humid rainforests

on the windy plains

in the echoing caves

the dark oases

the starstudded savannahs,

in the nights of snow and ice

we have kept the fire.

Women

have always been

the keepers of the fire.

This is not a memory.

It is a prayer.

⁂

It has not been very long

that we have lived for very long.

It has not been very long

in the long epochs of human history

that we have, any of us, had abundant food, electricity, medicines to give our young; that we have been spared long hours of chewing leather, softening bark, scraping hides, twisting plant fibers

to clothe ourselves and our loved ones.

Not very long at all since any of us

could read and write and see the opalescent earth

from 30,000 feet;

send songs across continents

draw water

effortlessly.

It has not been very long

that these wonders have been possible.

They have been made possible in a context so brutal

it has buried

whole peoples

whole languages

and wonders even greater than these have been extinguished in our genes.

It has not been very long

since we have even been able to look up from our fires

and see

that the fire is tended

through acrid fumes of kerosene

in the highlands of the Andes;

tended with dung, with brush, with laboriously gathered branches

in Africa

in Australia;

fires tended over gas stoves in the ghettoes of our cities.

It has not been very long since we have seen the flame

surrounded in the loins of women

varicolored;

heard it

leap to their tongues

in a thousand languages.

This is not a prayer.

This is a warning, daughter,

to the women of our race:

that if we would lift from our fires

the torches that will burn away our longing

we must gather in the night of our oppression

with all women

or there will not be light sufficient to dispel it

nor heat sufficient to kill and cremate this patriarchal tyranny of millenia.

We must be sure that the brand we lift from our fires

is not the body of an African child

not the arm of a Salvadoran peasant

the torso of an Iraqi girl.

It is we who have abundant food; our children spared with the new medicines; we who contemplate the earth from the stratosphere; we who broadcast our songs so loud they drown out

worldsong.

Our fires are big and hot

and we are deceived by their light;

deceived by the noise we are making ourselves.

We alone do not tend the fire; the fuel for our struggle, the gas and electricity and cars and paper and computers and health and money and

time

are resources stolen

from other women

without whom all our agitation

will come to nothing.

To evolve as a feminist, beyond a simple awareness that we are made to suffer because we are women and to desire to do something about it, we have to search for what we have in common as women, and what we have in common, as bell hooks has noted, transcends by far simply being angry with men.

Searching for this common ground

we must look at what separates us;

study the territory

over which we must build bridges.

Racism and patriarchy are as locked around our flesh as the African diamonds we wear to signify that our sex and our woman's labor is the exclusive property of one man. These are diamonds dredged in the blood of white supremacy by black men whose wives and mothers and sisters and lovers tend their cookfires unadorned with the fiery jewels of their own continent,

women whose fire aches and burns in them

for they are not permitted

to join their men

as they mine

symbols

of remote engagements.

Racism and patriarchy thrive upon one another and they take protective coloration from each other in ways which confuse and divide us deeply. Today, on the body economic where we have to defeat male supremacy (in the whole economy of our survival), there is no gangrene of patriarchy which is not deeply embedded in the wounds of racism. One cannot be amputated without amputating the other.

We should look at this

and be delighted,

not dismayed.

We should look at this

by the light of the fire we have always kept

and take out our kitchen knives

and carve the heart out of this whole economic system

with the lightheartedness

we have always felt

anticipating a good meal for the children.

There is no issue which separates us from the selves we seek to liberate from their gender prisons which doesn't also separate us from women of color.

We have come to realize, for example, that patriarchy has pinioned us on excruciating standards of beauty;

that we have been forced to measure our human selves

by the width of our butts

and the length of our noses:

that patriarchy has reduced us to meat

bought and sold over the counters of the supermarkets

over the spit-stained city streets

over the altars of churches;

that patriarchy has made of marriage itself

a form of prostitution.

When you wake up you realize that this ugly standard of "beauty" nourished in the masturbatory fantasies of power drunken men

has not only pinioned us

it has murdered black women.

Eliminated them, entirely.

For bad as it is,

it is a standard of ugliness white women at least have an illusion of achieving.

We have to come to terms with the fact that black women hate us for this. For while we didn't create it, we bought it,

hook, line, and sinker.

rushing into the dimestores and the emporiums and the beauty shops avidly plucking our hair out of our skin, painting and burning and dusting ourselves with chemicals, deforming our feet and our wombs, bathing ourselves in the stink of the corporate lotions in a real frenzy

to affirm this pale, wormy image

of white beauty.

Never mind for a moment that in this way we tell ourselves:

"We are ugly."

Black women are being told:

"You are hopelessly ugly."

Black women continue to have the TV hair of shaved rubber white women tossed at their faces in slow motion insult

day after day.

Some black men turn away from them.

Not to us, not to who we really are

but to white power pork chops.

I have been in communities of people of color so remote from whites that they had never seen blue eyes—communities where my eyes were stared into so openly, for such duration, that I was reduced to exhaustion,

and hanging in the huts of those people via the earth penetrating tentacles of the Coca Cola Corporation

were the bodies of white women contorted like sausages on flyspecked calendars,

their minds crushed out of their faces for the photographer

or blown away with an airbrush.

What kind of contact could I seek with those women

who had been staring at those calendars, too;

who had been watching their men stare at those calendars for years;

women whose minds had not been crushed out of their faces

and who had no other experience

to associate me with.

At the butcher store over there at the intersection

of racism and patriarchy

our bodies have been made not only meat,

but white meat,

symbols of white power

dangled before men of color

who are invited in this way to believe

that the acquisition, conquest, purchase, or display

of a white female

confers some white power on them;

or at the very least,

defies the supremacy of white males.

At the butcher store over there at the intersection

of racism and patriarchy

the bodies of black males have been made into

black meat

symbols of male power

dangled before white women

who are invited in this way to believe

that the acquisition, conquest, purchase or display

of a black male

confers some female power on them;

or at the very least,

defies the supremacy of white males.

At the butcher store over there at the intersection

of racism and patriarchy

the bodies of black women

are on sale very cheap

so cheap that black men, white women and men are invited to believe that

they are dogfood.

It's time to boycott the butcher store.

It's time to join black women

who have never bought anything in that store.

Who have never entertained illusions

that there is

any power

to be bought in that store

for anybody.

If we would reclaim our beauty

we need to recognize theirs.

Their beauty has always been

the banner of the boycott.

This question of beauty, which has so alienated us from ourselves, has driven a stake between us and women of color. There is much more to it, of course. Even this cursory peek into the labyrinths of racism and patriarchy is too simple. Love has emerged in unions of all colors and genders. I only want to point out that their probability and some of their consequences have been poisoned.

But what separates us most deeply from black women are not the sexual fantasies of men sick from power or sick for power or even our complicity in those fantasies; it is the blood of children.

Annals of history record that the American slave ship Pongas carried 250 women, many of them pregnant, who were squeezed into a compartment of 16 by 18 feet. The women who survived the initial stages of pregnancy gave birth aboard ship with their bodies exposed to either the scorching sun or the freezing cold. The numbers of black women who died during childbirth or the number of stillborn children will never be known....Often the slavers brutalized children to watch the anguish of their mothers. In their personal account of life aboard a slave ship, the Weldons recounted an incident in which a child of nine months was flogged continuously for refusing to eat. When beating failed to force the child to eat, the captain ordered that the child be placed feet first into a pot of boiling water. After trying other torturous methods with no success, the captain dropped the child and caused its death. Not deriving enough satisfaction from this sadistic act, he then commanded the mother to throw the body of the child overboard. The mother refused but was beaten until she submitted. (bell hooks, 18-19)

Slavery meant more than chains and whip and brutal labor in the fields to black women, because they were slaves in the whole human economy. "The black male slave was primarily exploited as a laborer in the fields; the black female was exploited as a laborer in the fields, a worker in the domestic household, a breeder, and as an object of white male sexual assault" (22)

Slavery meant the systematic sexual abuse of black women, who could be raped into multiple pregnancies from the age of thirteen and on to an early death, literally forced to "breed" profits for whites. When they gave birth, whether from rape or a desired union, their children could be ripped away from them and sold. These were childworkers who could not know from one breath to another whether their children would be sold away from them forever; who watched their little girls raped by white boys and white men; watched their little boys whipped, kicked, yanked away from their fires, whose job it was to prepare their children, not for life, but for continual death.

What separates us most deeply from black women today is the vastly different nature of our childwork, as black women, all women of color, must socialize their children into survival of a very different kind than the one we know.

·⁓⋐⋑⋏·

Slavery offered some white women a way out of the endless rounds of drudgery their lives as women were defined by. Women who had never had a moment's rest in their lives could now be surrounded by servants. In that sense, the economics of patriarchy in their lives made slavery an attractive institution.

White women steeped in the terror of sex which was the great cultural landmark of their Christian culture; who were brainwashed into believing that sex was evil, that their own female sexuality was the eternal curse of Eve, the downfall of humankind; who believed that men were the innocent victims of female seduction; that men were raging animals unable to control their lust at the sight of a woman's ankle,

knew their men raping the black girls in their very houses

and turned viciously against those black girls

for the crime of

"seducing"

their men.

Had them sold, beaten, turned out again into the fields, beat them themselves. Took vengeance on the black women in a thousand ways.

⋅⊶⋅

You have to understand how intimate slavery was to understand the intimacy of racism. White women saw black women bear children with their own features, their fathers' features, their brothers'—saw their brothers and sisters sold away; were anxious to see their blood brothers and sisters sold away from their sight.

Children could ask who their father was

and when the black mother

pointed to their father,

look and see a whip coming down on them.

This is patriarchy

in its most naked form.

⋅⊶⋅

This isn't remote. This was only yesterday. There are black women alive today whose great-grandmothers were slaves. And none of this has changed in essence; it has only mutated in form. The slaves were never completely freed. Their chains were only lengthened to accomodate their own increasing rebellion and an economy which made less overt forms of subjugating their labor more profitable.

The social relations between white women and black women are no less tortuous today for being less visible.

⋅⊶⋅

The women's movement in the U.S. was born in the fight against slavery. The women abolitionists were forced to organize themselves because their men would not even let them speak publicly. It was a movement that blossomed into a revolutionary power in the 19th century as white women joined black women, first against slavery, and then in the struggle for suffrage.

And the women's movement, as an organized power, crumpled into a white ladies' reform movement, largely ineffectual for a century, when the white women betrayed the black women over the issue of the black man's right to vote. After years of labor campaigning against slavery, and for women's suffrage, women saw black men given the vote, while all women remained disenfranchised. Rather than seeing this as a measure of progress, and continuing their campaign, the white women were terrified. Ignorant and demoralized, they openly decried this as an insult, not just to their gender, but to their race, the only "educated" race. The vote, they felt, should be given to "educated" people, those who were "civilized." They felt insulted that "uncivilized, half savage" black men should get the vote, and not "educated" white women like themselves. Black women, glad to see their men get the vote, and anxious to get it themselves, could not join this racist protest.

What's more, white women opportunistically closed ranks against the black women in order to win support of white women in the south. They felt that they were fighting for their lives, that any expedient was justified. These women didn't understand the suicidal nature of racism, nor did they understand how degrading, suffocating and sterile was their own white Victorian "education." This pathetic, ignorant stampede for that illusory symbol of their freedom, the vote, over the backs of the black women, gained them nothing. The first women to get the vote were both black *and* white.

·☙❧·

Meanwhile, through this white ignorance, the most revolutionary organized movement which had ever emerged for the liberation of women was destroyed. That doesn't mean that there was no struggle, by individuals and groups, black and white, during the century that followed, but it was never again so powerful until the middle of the 20th century, when it emerged, *again* on the wings of the movement for black liberation in the 1960s, which was called the Civil Rights movement. This was no accident.

And the narrowminded focus of some white women on gender oppression—as if gender were separate from race—again forced women of color into the impossible position of joining a racist protest for their freedom. They will always, always, choose for their families.

·☙❧·

The conditions under which most women childwork in this country are so bad that the conflicts inherent to childwork are magnified into bizarre proportions. Even a middle class white woman is forced to brutalize her child's integrity and common sense into the pinched abstractions of private property:

forced to make it somehow "normal" that those trees are for climbing

but those trees over there are a no-no, they "belong" to somebody;

you can play with these rocks,

but you can't touch those rocks, those rocks are private landscape rocks.

Children have a lot of trouble with all these invisible boundaries. They fail to see the earth as an infinitely divisible piece of real estate.

This creates a lot of conflict between them and their childworkers.

A black woman, or any woman of color,

is forced to prune her child's sense of freedom

much earlier, much more thoroughly, and much deeper into the core of her child's humanity.

There is no labor

harder than this

in all of human experience.

There is no daily work that any men do anywhere so drenched in anguish.

⁂

It seems to me one of the most stunning achievements of human labor ever wrought

beside which pyramids and cathedrals and moonrockets pale

is embodied in the insouciant, laughing beauty preserved in those children.

⁂

A white child can join together with his white friends and go roaring down the street on a skateboard and the white childworker has to worry about him getting hit by a car; or the aftereffects on Mrs. Smith's geranium hedge, but when a black or brown child gets together with his black friends, it is more likely to be called a gang, and the black childworker has to worry about him being shot to death by a white policeman or, indeed, a gang member.

·☙❧·

It isn't only relations with black women we need to understand and change. There are relations between ourselves and Mexican women, Asian women, Native American women, with similar contours but very specific histories. (Native Americans, who were the only people with any authentic claim to this land whatsoever, did not get the vote until 1924, men *or* women).

And while racism has provided white women with stereotypes of black women, evil sexual Jezebels, and fat, forgiving mammies,

racism has given black women stereotypes of us, as well. Reading the work of black women, I bridle at the constant portrayal of white women as despotic aristocrats bullying their servants. I worked for years as a maid in motels and as a maid in houses of women white like myself. The vast majority of white women do not have servants and those who do are not uniformly evil, power-crazed witches.

It angers me when black women portray us all as bitches screaming rape, anxious to have black men lynched. Less than a third of lynchings ever even involved allegations of rape, and the majority of those allegations were made by white men—when it was white men who smoked up the rape issue to murder behind, not white women. The majority of white women do not even live in the south; do not have grandmothers or great-grandmothers who were slaveowners or who ever even lived in the slave states.

Things are not so simple.

and yet, in a way,

they are.

The whole truth is permeated with the forces behind the stereotypes they have of us. This cannot be said of the stereotypes we have of them. Even if we have no direct historical relations with the south, or with the slave trade, the fact is that we are the beneficiaries of white privilege, whether we have sought it or not.

·☙❧·

The specific histories and explorations of the separations between ourselves and women of color are extensive, but what I want to do here is point out their centrality in achieving the unity and vision to free us all as women—and to underline the great danger of being deluded into believing, as Sandra Harding wrote, that

> As a social institution, designed and controlled by men, ...the vast panorama of the history of race relations becomes one more male drama in which the more powerful group of men works out its infantile project of dominating the other. Race relations are fundamentally social relations between men, where women find themselves supporting characters or, occasionally, thrust forward to leading roles in a script they have not written and cannot direct. (153)

This is not an argument of feminists.

This is an argument made by ladies who are afraid of their responsibility.

Women are not helpless.

White women spit on the black children boarding the buses in Boston, in New Orleans;

white women have stood by and jeered on the lynchings of black men;

there are many white women who teach their children to fear and distrust people of color.

Men indeed bear the greatest responsibility for the creation and maintenance of the economic system in which we find ourselves crushed

but we have colluded in all the forms of these male dominated oppressions

including our oppression as women

in ways well within our control.

If we want free ourselves, we can't push our responsibilities, lesser though they may be, on to men.

·⊱⊰·

If we were closer to women of color, we would see that all the man questions which have been defined as "women's issues" are infinitely more oppressive to them than they are to us. They have the most pressing need for education; for the right to abortions; the most acute childwork problems; the heaviest shitwork burdens in poor housing; the least access to decent employment; are the most vulnerable to rape; to entrapment in prostitution prison; carry the heaviest burden as emotional workers; as caretakers of the sick and aged.

In some places they are subject to forms of involuntary sterilization. They are on the front lines. If we join them, share our resources, speak to racist oppression as well as gender oppression, fill the space between us with such oxygen, we might blast through the obstacles frustrating us with a burst of released womanfire, the likes of which nobody has ever seen.

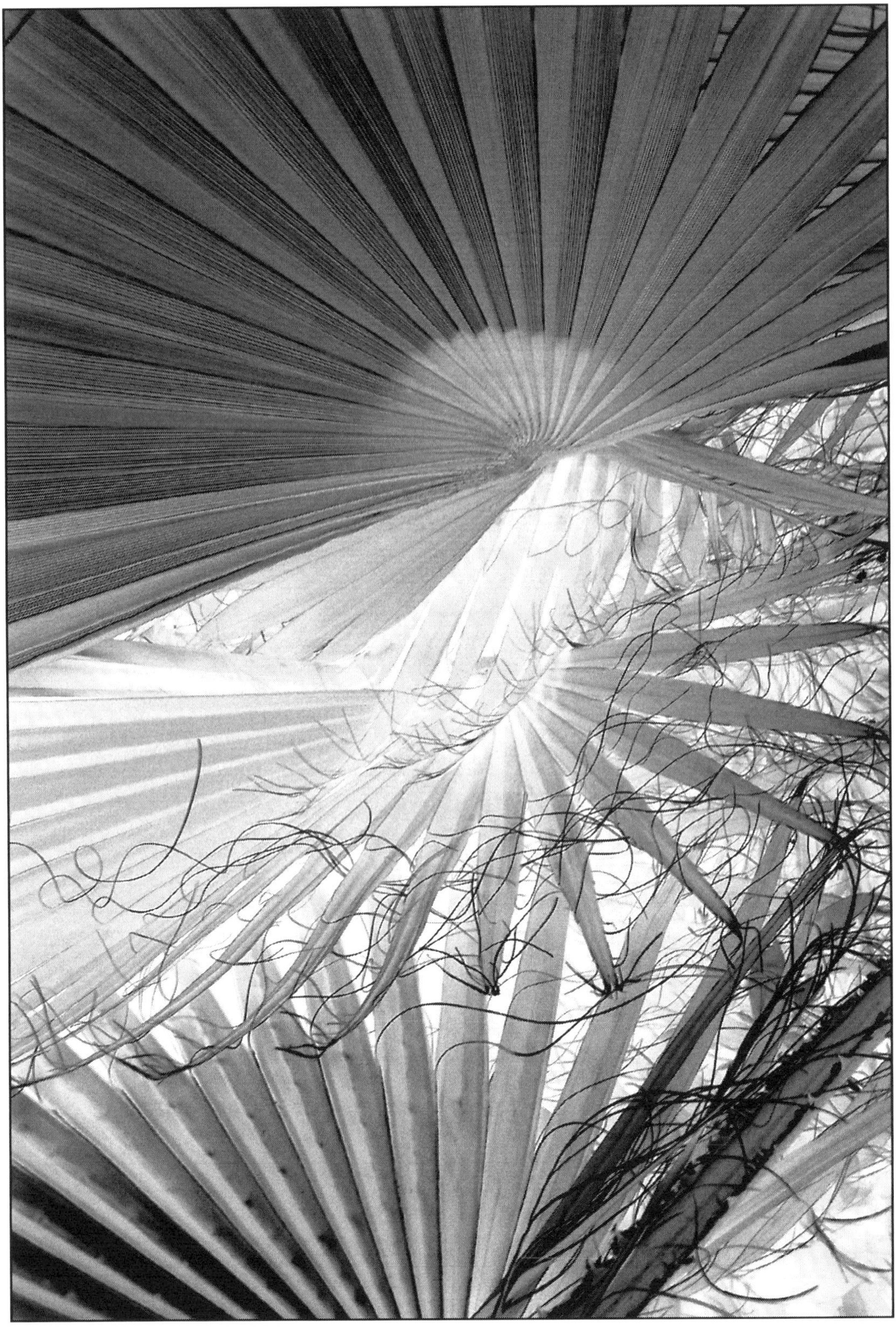

CHAPTER IX

The Mirror Effect

There is another wave penetrating the fields of all these forces

but frequently obscured in the maelstrom of their meeting

which is purely patriarchal.

It travels through the medium of class.

It's important to recognize because it's another barrier between women, another mode for women to hate women.

·⁂·

It is easy enough to see how class divides women.

Class differences are common to women *and* men.

Here I refer to a much less understood effect of class, which is an often unexamined process involving the oppression of women purely as women. It takes some of its most acute forms in a way correlated to the degree of power wielded by their men.

I don't mean that women of the upper classes are the most oppressed women in the world, by any means, but there is something going on in patriarchy

as it pounds through the hierarchies of class

which we would do well to study.

·⁂·

It was the wives of the feudal lords of China who had their feet bound into stumps, not women of the fields.

It was women of the highest levels of European aristocracy who were forced to bear idiots;

wives of the bourgeoisie of the industrial revolution bound breathless into their corsets upon whom fell the "responsibility" to organize charitable institutions to wipe up with their skirts the blood their men were squeezing out of the children in the factories, women who were supposed to function as their men's "conscience."

Mrs. Winchester silently going mad, building room after room onto her mansion, long after her husband's death, to house the ghosts of those murdered by his rifles. (This house is still standing in the town where you were born. As an architectural expression of such a woman's psyche, it is unique in the world).

In our society, upper class women are still expected to function as their men's "conscience";

still the women of the upper classes who are most completely objectified into garish displays of men's wealth, maintained at great expense in spas, beauty salons, drug and alcohol clinics.

It is in the upper classes that women who have made use of their educational opportunities are still expected to function as "hostesses," to use the skills they acquired with their advanced college degrees arranging platters of finger food.

I was struck with the bitter irony of this "mirror effect" as a little girl.

My father enlisted in the army as a buck private, and as we traveled, and he frequently abandoned us, my mother could go to the army and complain and eventually they would garnish some pittance out of his wages to keep us alive

but when he became an officer and he abandoned us,

the army wouldn't garnish his wages any more.

He was "an officer and a gentleman," now

and his wages could no longer be garnished.

This is the real meaning of being "an officer and a gentleman."

When he beat her bloody, breaking her body against the walls,

nobody came. None of the other officers and gentlemen hearing her screams in the officer and gentlemens' housing complex we lived in

came. They would wait. Scurry over and put her on their shoulders in a blanket and carry her to the hospital like a bag

only after he left,

to avoid embarassing

another officer and gentleman.

In Germany, when the beatings became so severe she tried to leave, she was told she could only return to the United States if she had two hundred dollars

for each of her children. So we wouldn't become "wards of the state."

The only place she could get two hundred dollars each for my brother and me, was from my father.

She could go, the army said. But if she didn't have that money,

she would have to leave me and my brother behind.

Patriarchy has a million ways of saying to women, "Your children or your life."

Of course, he would not give it to her.

A family is an important accouterment to an officer and a gentleman.

It would have reflected badly on his career.

Even as a young girl, I pondered on this paradox:

that the more power he had

the less we had.

While the plight of women of the upper classes is not the most urgent priority in the world, it is misleading to lump women into the same economic class as their husbands. Many white women remain quietly trapped in their marriages precisely because they do not belong to the same economic class as their husbands do

and if they have children

they do so having pragmatically calibrated the relative impact, on themselves and their children, of the oppression of private patriarchy versus the oppression of public patriarchy.

This is particularly true in what is considered the white "middle class," which, objectively, is a class dominated by men.

A couple who own a house, for example, may be "equal" before the divorce laws, but even if the entire house were left to the woman, at 79 cents to the dollar earning power, or less, there may be no way a woman alone can maintain the house, pay taxes and insurance on it, heat it, light it, de-termite it, water its greenery.

In fact, many women in this position discover that they cannot even get the credit necessary to buy insurance

in fact, most middle class divorces take place around mortgaged houses and unpaid for cars

in fact, the only way that divorce does not impoverish a "middle class" woman is if the couple actually own some income producing property which can be divided between them, and this puts people in a much higher class than even most professionals belong to, a very small class indeed

in fact, many white women so vocal in the women's movement are not so middle of the middle class at all.

It is misleading to lump women into the class their husbands belong to as well, because the power dynamics of patriarchy create a marked tendency for white women to marry up (in class) and men to marry down. Under patriarchy, relative helplessness in a woman is attractive to a man. So that within the gradations of a given class, and frequently in movements across classes, there is a natural channel for white women who want to have children to be "rescued" up in. It is not so unusual for a white woman from the working class to be found in a marriage with a middle class man, especially if she fits patriarchal standards of "beauty," and very unusual for the opposite to occur.

The class status of men is not defined by marriage, but they always feel more secure living with a woman whose earning power and/or educational achievements are inferior to theirs. So that even within many marriages, class outlook, class values, and class itself, clash.

·⁓⁓·

In addition to this very real economic bondage, there is another factor in the gender oppression of these women which makes it subjectively excruciating, and that is, education. For the more educated they become about their real status, the more agonizing are their efforts to maintain their self esteem. And this is true, not only in the dimension of their status as women, but in their status as humans who are afforded opportunities for higher education in all fields,

even if those opportunities extend no higher than the local community college

and are given no chance for their knowledge and skills to be either recognized or rewarded in any way which objectively betters their lives.

A little larnin' is a dangerous thing, all right.

I don't think it is suprising at all that the movement for women's liberation should flare up so brightly at precisely that fissure in this racist, patriarchal, capitalist, geography where so-called "middle class" white women find their lives suspended.

·⁓⁓·

It is important to understand those women because we are constantly invited to ridicule them. All forms of woman-hating are patriarchal, reactionary, and defeat us all. It is one thing to be aware of the class bias reflected in the attitudes of those women, and to fight against it, but it is a different thing altogether to subject them to sneers and contempt as women. It's also important to understand their perspective because their objective position in the power structures we seek to overthrow lends a truly revolutionary potential to their struggle.

Demeaned and ignored, they can indeed become a mob banging their pots and pans for facism, but under other circumstances, they were found at the front lines in Managua, serving food from their kitchens to the boychildren of the barricades—and this is nothing compared to the damage they can wreak on the existing power structures if we would learn to understand the race and class transcending nature of gender as an advantage, learn to see it a a weapon, rather than as a source of discouragement,

if we would address them as women

and stop addressing them as appendages of their men.

   Since you have never been

   buried in veils,

   beaten,

   your labor or your body bartered

   in the invisible markets of male prestige

   and, if you have so far escaped being raped,

   you will find it hard, as a young woman

   filled with the promise of the world

   to evaluate or even find credible

   the crippling power of the patriarchy.

   In the early stages of the journey,

   the paths which follow men

   are verdant and deep as rain forests.

   Dense with their own perfume

   young women dream themselves

   into the arms of men

   grow pregnant with the beauty of those dreams

   bear them like blossoms of fire

and never again emerge.

You need not be cautious in your dreaming.

Be cautious only of your fire,

that you may warm

all the dreams of your creation

by the incandescent light of your being

and not in its immolation.

❦

One place where you can investigate the uncanny strength of these forces and observe them, experimentally, let's say, without being consumed

(now, while you are young)

is at their most vulnerable juncture.

Being the most vulnerable,

it is by far the most trivialized

but don't be fooled.

This is in the area of the dishrag and the broom.

❦

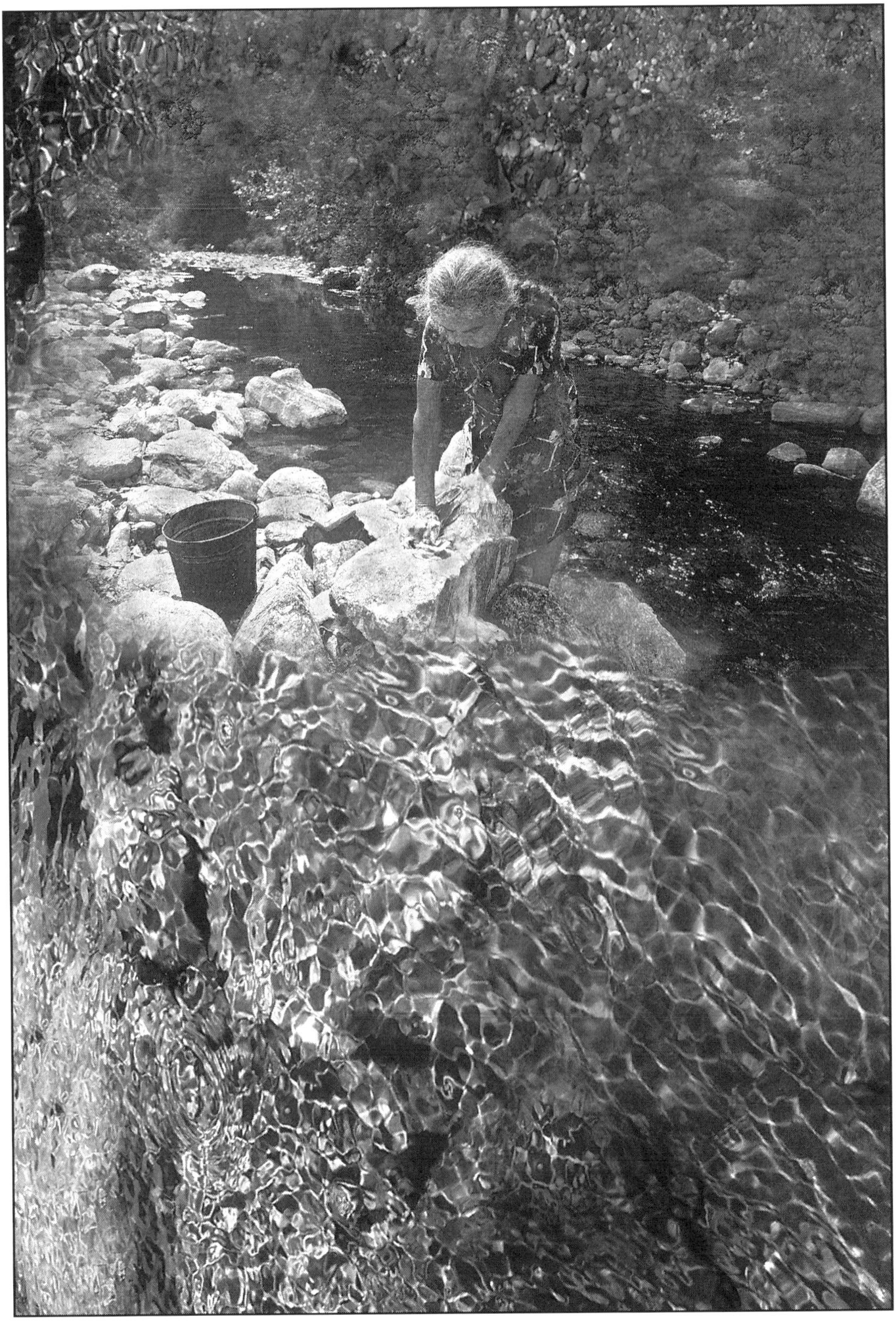

CHAPTER X

The Shitwork Factor

All of the domestic labor women are expected to perform is peripheral to the central patriarchal division of labor which gives women exclusive responsibility for childwork. This has the effect of making all women mothers to all men throughout their lifetimes, whether a woman has ever borne a child or not. The shitwork flows out of this central division of labor like a concentric wave: it is not the cause of our oppression, but incidental to it.

It's easy to see, historically, why this is so. Children create lots of messy incidents. Early on it was women who remained closest to camp. This work became identified with women and as patriarchy took hold, was extrapolated to encompass all domestic work and frozen into an obligation, a mandatory bow to male privilege. Moreover, all children themselves grow up seeing women and only women clean up after them. As usual, patriarchy is reinforced both ways, internally and externally.

It isn't simply the case that women are identified with cooking and cleaning, either. Men identify their very masculinity with having it done for them. It is so oppressive, I have been tempted not to teach you how to cook, because it will only be held against you.

Of course you must learn to cook, to eat and to share food with pleasure, but don't learn to cook for men. For the sake of illustration, however, I include the following sketch.

·⁂·

"Daughter do not learn to cook for men
as it will only be held against you"

Learn instead to make music. If all the hours you would otherwise spend for men in markets and kitchens are spent learning to control, say, a guitar, you may become a fine, competent musician.

Let men take care of their own animal necessities. They may learn, as we have learned and relearned over millenia, that they (as well as we) are animals as well as humans. It might give them some humility and make them more bearable.

Housework of any kind, for a man, won't ennoble you. It will only brutalize you. Don't betray yourself. Don't do it as "a favor this one time." It is not a favor, to you or to them.

Don't do it out of pity for their (real) suffering. Their (real) suffering is neither caused by their shitwork nor alleviated by your doing it.

Don't do it out of exhaustion with their (feigned) incompetence.

Don't do it out of an (oppressed) sense of justice that since they (as men) (it isn't their fault) are more powerful in the world, their (good) work can bring about positive results, yours is not recognized, therefore not effective at this (always) critical juncture in (his)story so you will be making a more valuable contribution by freeing up (his) time.

Don't do it out of impatience (They are counting on this).

Don't do it out of habit. It is a vicious habit which will pollute your soul and theirs.

Don't do it out of love. It will kill your love for them.

Don't do it for their approval. It is a source of contempt for women.

Don't do it out of fear. Free, you are as powerful as they.

Don't do it out of convenience. It will never be convenient for them to do it. It will always be convenient for you to do it.

Don't do it for a man's ego (how humiliating for his friends to see him doing this; they are not as 'advanced' as he, they will not understand; you don't wish to undermine his status with others).

You'll only undermine your own ego and your own status and demonstrate to him that the status quo must be preserved.

Don't do it to please his parents or your parents or any elderly people who are threatened by this "offense" to their sense of order, no matter how much affection you have for them, no matter how dearly you want their approval. Affection and approval predicated on your oppression are tools to bludgeon you back into submission. Accept only affection and approval predicated on respect for you.

Does he hold you tenderly in his arms at night after you have spent an entire day elaborately cooking, cleaning, and washing, and whisper, "You are a good Woman."

Does he melt down and stroke you while you are chopping vegetables?

   Watch out.

He has been conditioned down to his very bones to reward you for negating yourself and to attack, trivialize, and exile you from his affections if you don't.

   And you are human and long to be stroked.

Don't try to win the love of a man (if it's love from a man you seek) by picking up his shoes, wiping his beard hairs out of the sink, preparing his meals. The affection this earns is the same as that given a dog who goes for the newspaper.

Don't do it to comfort him. If he needs comfort, he can listen to music.

Don't do it "temporarily" because he is having (real) difficulties in his life right now. His life, like your life, like everyone's lives, will always be full of real difficulties.

Don't do it "temporarily" because he has negotiated some tit for tat arrangement with you whereby he will do it at some future (minute; hour; day; week; year). This can be the most frustrating illusion of all because it exploits your sense of "fairness." What you will discover is that:

   a) you will be put in the position of enforcing his side of the "bargain" (nag);

   b) he may (grudgingly) do some of his own shitwork but never all of it, and never on time, and never well, and never without resentment;

   c) while you fulfill your part of this "bargain" by doing his shitwork and your own, he may (grudgingly) do some of his own shitwork but never all of it and never on time and never well and never without resentment and never, never, any of yours.

   Studies have been done of couples who consider themselves "liberated." The man will be asked if he participates in the housework and "does his share." Proudly he will answer yes. The woman will be asked if he participates in the housework and "does his share" and proudly (She has gained a few inches. She is proud.) she answers yes. But when the chores, and the time required to do them are analyzed according to what he (proudly) actually does and what she actually does, in 80% of the cases she is doing between 60 and 90% of the work.

Don't be deceived that because he is (oh, admirable) doing something, he is liberated, you are liberated, he is "doing his share."

His share will always be smaller than your share. What these studies reveal is understandable. If you have never had freedom, and you get a little bit of it, that little bit seems like a big deal indeed.

·⁂·

Don't do it so that he can rest. Very few men value rest. Even fewer know how to rest. This may be one reason they don't live as long as women.

As a woman, you will see this and (watch out) take pity on him.

It is his responsibility to program his life so that it includes rest, not yours. Your rest is as important as his rest.

Don't do it because you "are better at it" than he is. Of course you are. But with experience, and only with experience, will he learn.

Don't do it because "it's so easy." (He's not asking you to do something difficult, is he? It doesn't require that much effort, just to pick up that one little cup, does it? How silly can you get?)

It requires your *time*. Your time is your life. If it is so easy, so trivial, so unimportant in the Grand Scheme of Things, then why can't he do it? If it's "not much," then why is he even arguing about it?

Don't do it because his work is more important than yours. The work that a person does is that person's life. His life is not more important than your life, no matter what you choose or are forced to choose to do with your life.

Don't do it because he makes more money than you do. Men always make more money than women. That is a primary component of our oppression, not something to be ashamed of. It is not your fault.

Don't stop doing it as though you were a worker on strike. A strike is a temporary phenomenon. Striking is a last resort to force the boss to negotiate with you.

He is not the boss.

There is no reward you can negotiate with him if you have put yourself in this position. (His affection for you as a subordinate? His money? A brief vacation from his oppression?) that can equal the value of your own time, your own life.

Just don't negotiate about it at all.

Do not do it at all.

It's that simple.

Don't do it at all, under any circumstances, for any reason, and you'll be free of it.

Don't negotiate your freedom with a man.

Do not ask men to make you free.

Make yourself free.

·⁓❦⁓·

Now, what will happen? Depending on the man, what happens can escalate to various places on a negative behavioral scale. For example,

he will sulk.

Become petulant.

Become very, very busy with other things.

Withdraw love. (Watch out. If you have to be his drudge to qualify for his love, he doesn't want you).

Try desperately to "reason" (negotiate) with you. (Watch out.) You are going to get exhausted with all this tension and be tempted to negotiate so that you both can "be happy again" as if you (both) ever were.

He panics. He loses his composure. He appeals to your (male-defined) sense of justice. He hopes it will all go away if he waits long enough.

When all else has failed, when he realizes that you will not negotiate, his panic may assume enormous proportions.

The spectacle of a fellow human undergoing panic is unnerving. You can't help but feel compassion. (Watch out).

You will also find it hard not to be infected with panic yourself, because panic is contagious. (Wouldn't it just be easier and safer and more comfortable and less destructive to just do this one tiny insignificant chore for him and relieve you both...)

Watch out. That one, tiny, insignificant chore is absolute capitulation back into negotiability. It tells him that there are limits to what you can endure for your freedom. It tells him that this threat to his sense of self is real and you can be counted on, in the end, to rescue him from the panic he experiences when confronting his own responsibilities.

Faced with the necessity to prepare his own food and clean up after himself indefinitely, he becomes cowardly and irrational.

He is convinced that the world is coming to an end and his enactment of this deep (very real) conviction will threaten your own sense of what is going on and your own sense of stability and reason.

His panic is truly contagious because it is based on the truth. It is not a fantasy. The world is coming to an end. The world as he knows it and expects it to be. The world of male dominance and female submission.

O.K. You have not capitulated. You have not negotiated. Steadfastly you have gone about doing your own work. Steadfastly you have gone about resting your own rest. You have weathered his descent into the state of being a nervous wreck without becoming one yourself.

Now what happens?

Now in the case of some men, it can get very serious.

His resentment at you for not fulfilling his expectations of you as Woman; his betrayed authority; his growing sense of helplessness at your refusal to reason (negotiate) with him can begin to emerge in increasingly ugly forms.

If you did not appreciate just how degrading, grotesque, and ugly sexism was before, just watch it play itself out in his psyche; in his facial expressions.

He attacks.

These attacks take many forms but they have the character of becoming increasingly overt.

He calls you a bitch.

The word "bitch" means "female dog."

He thinks you are a female dog because he has always treated women as though they were dogs. Women have always been submissive, haven't they? Man(ageable). Watch out. It hurts to be called an animal. It hurts to be called a cat (women are "catty"). It hurts to be called a hen (women who gather socially are having "hen" parties"). It hurts very, very much to be called a bitch when you are fighting for your time (your life).

No matter how clearly you understand what is going on, no matter how intellectually you are prepared for it, it's going to sink into your heart like a sharp rock. It's going to hurt bad.

Since you are a human, and not an animal, there is no way for you to avoid this pain. Be strong. Don't try to find some way to wound him equally in return. There is no epithet to describe males even remotely equivalent to the word "bitch" as it is used to describe women. The very fact that this is so is eloquent testimony to the power of patriarchy.

Anyone who thinks you are a dog is very confused.

Men have been confused for a long, long time.

I know it's hard to do, but you have to step back and let him flail away at this fantasy. Don't try to wound him back. He doesn't know what he's fighting. (He thinks it's a dog).

He doesn't know why you are not submissive to his sense of how things should be. He thinks you can have a perfectly good life with Things As They Are. (He has never experienced your oppression).

He doesn't know himself as an oppressor. (He thinks he is a very nice guy).

He is terrified of losing your love. (He thinks that all this means you don't love him).

Don't slash back because he isn't fighting you. He's fighting his own fantasies of what women are and because he's fighting something which doesn't exist, any response on his level is (a) futile; (b) reaffirms his sense that he is fighting a real (dog) and; (c) is extremely dangerous.

Steadfastly go about doing your own work and resting your own rest.

You are going to need it because you are about to be presented with the most exquisite male fantasy of them all:

He accuses you (snarling: watch that body language) of trying to dominate him.

This is the grandest and most pathetic confusion. Even when you are prepared for it, it is flabbergasting, the most stunning bomb in the arsenal of sexist ideas. Not the most stunning in terms of the pain it can cause you, but the most stunning in its outright, unabashed stupidity.

It is also the most laughable.

But don't laugh. He is confused.

He is a wounded man. He has been so amputated of feeling (by patriarchy), so alienated (by patriarchy) from the (potent)ial of real human love based on the respect that flows out of mutual freedom, that he believes this dog and master relationship (whatever "liberal" version of it he insists on) is love.

He has never known anything else, and doesn't intuit reward in anything else.

Men, too, are the victims of patriarchy.

Don't retreat an inch in your rejection of his sexism, but don't reject him. Don't gratuitiously stab him back. Don't demand his blood. His blood and your freedom are very different things. Slashing him with your anger (and you are angry. oh god are you angry) will not give you your freedom. He didn't invent patriarchy. Anger is to save for release in an organized way, against the institutions of patriarchy at a political level where it can do some good.

Don't heed his call to you as a female dog by lunging at his throat. He knows no other version of relations between men and women except the male dominant one. It is natural that he feels that overthrowing these relations can only mean reversing them. He imagines (and this is only his imagination, but he doesn't know it. He is confused.)—he imagines being dominated. And by a woman, yet, that most contemptible of genders! And he rises up, flooded with adrenalin, to protect his integrity.

Beneath the roles that patriarchy has forced us into, women search for real love and men search for real love. Don't be put off by this grotesque mask of sexism he wears, even in the heat of his attacks.

There is a human love behind it seeking your human love.

He has never experienced life as a woman and your oppression is not real to him.

There is nothing you can do about his illusions. You will never be able to talk him out of them. You can talk until you are blue in the face.

In fact, he will welcome such talk after a while.

It occupies time that he doesn't need to use washing dishes; it makes him appear reasonable; it makes him appear liberated.

And best of all, it puts your refusal to do his shitwork on the table (from which he is not obliged to rise) where it can (and will) assume the dimensions of something that can be bargained around.

If you are "willing to discuss" it with him, then you will be drawn into discussion. In a discussion, anyone can disagree. He will, with indisputable (male) logic, disagree with your position.

He will *always* disagree with your position.

And there you are.

We all have disagreements, don't we?

It isn't his fault he doesn't agree with you.

You are a democratic person.
You can't force a person to do something they disagree with, right?

And there you are, back to square one, having been tricked back to the bargaining table where your freedom (your time, your life) will always constitute the biggest bargain men have ever had.

And it is late. Your very willingness to discuss it has robbed from you hours to attend to your own work, your own rest.

You are not responsible to educate your oppressor.

You will never reason a man out of his sexism because sexism isn't based on reason.

⁓⋅⋅⋅⁓

So what can you do?

Go steadfastly about your own work. Rest steadfastly your own rest.

He'll flail around in his fantasy. Let him pout and snarl and lunge and shout and grimace and slam doors and squeal tires and point fingers. (But don't allow him to strike you. This is the ultimate logic of sexism: loss of your life).

Go steadfastly about your own work. Rest steadfastly your own rest.

His state of mind will make this very difficult to do if your are living with him, but do it as best you can. Be loyal to yourself.

He will get tired eventually and give up. This will really happen. He'll get tired of flailing around with a ghost after a while and be forced to look at you. He will see you steadfastly doing your own work and resting your own rest. Most men have never seen a woman doing this. Sooner or later it will dawn on him that this is really what you want. Not any of the things he thinks you want (or should want). Not revenge, or power over him, but power over yourself.

Later yet, he'll realize that this makes you happy. And finally, he may realize that it makes him happy, too. He has never been happy as an oppressor. As a dominant male he has been led to believe that the happiness of women depends on him. And yet no matter what he does (and if he is a good man, he has tried very hard to fulfill the male version of what women want)

No matter how hard he busts ass to fulfill this (sexist, patriarchal, suffocating) male role that was handed to him in the crib,

those goddam women have never appreciated him. Have never appreciated how hard it is on him (and it is hard on him. It is inhuman.)

No matter how hard he tries, they keep on complaining, they keep on *bitching*!

He'll get tired. Stop and notice reality. This will really happen. Have faith in the laws of energy. You can sustain doing your own work and resting your own rest forever. He cannot sustain a state of rage and panic for very long, or even work himself up to it with any frequency if it is calmly demonstrated to him, over and over again, that there is no reward in it. He cannot bear to lose forever and since he is fighting with thin air, he can never win.

  Entropy is on your side.

⸙

What if, after all this, he still refuses to take responsibility for his own animal necessities and the byproducts of his own animal existence?

Get rid of him. He is a serious source of pollution.

In practice, you probably won't have to. In practice, men this terrified of themselves flee in search of another childworker. In practice, it's a valid test of whether a man is even worthy of your love.

Don't be afraid of his flight. If your respect for yourself is based on yourself, and not on men, you'll experience his absence as a great relief.

And don't worry about "finding another man." Life goes on very nicely without them. What's more, you and they will always "find" one another. It is women you need to work to "find." It is women with whom you can form relationships uncontaminated with these exhausting struggles to preserve your integrity. Women are not looking for a personal childworker, and when they look at you, that is not what they "see."

In community with women, you can endure anything

and you can achieve everything,

your time

your life

your freedom

⸙

  The Shitwork Factor is crucial, not trivial, because it takes away our time (our lives). Politically, the Shitwork Factor is a key to our liberation. This is because it is the weakest link in the chain of patriarchy fastened around our lives. It's the part of our bondage over which we have the most power, that is mostly enforced by us ourselves.

Gender oppression transcends class. Many people see this as a political obstacle. But what it means in terms of struggle is that we do have some personal, individual power to fight for our gender liberation. This doesn't mean that you or I can achieve liberation alone, but it does mean that we can *achieve some significant power over our individual lives*, merely by refusing, consistently, to do any shitwork for men.

Clearly, different women in different situations are able to do this in different degrees. For example, a woman who is married and whose children are economically dependent on a man may not be in a position to refuse to do it all, but she may be able to refuse to do some of it. All of a sudden she stops making the bed. Or declares that one night a week she will not fix dinner. Or iron his shirts, or wherever she calibrates is the best place. Every individual woman in each situation will know where this place is.

The shitwork factor is the weakest link in part because the revolution is already underway. There is already established a certain ideological respectability to men's "sharing" the work of cleaning up after themselves, feeding themselves, and so on.

A tremendous (telling) amount of tension will go down over the night off, the shirts, the bed, whatever. But in the end, the man will be likely to weigh all the other services the marriage provides and decide that in the balance, it's not worth losing the whole marriage over. If it is handled well, he will even achieve a certain amount of (justifiable) self-esteem proving himself "liberated."

Then she can push a little further.

What she will discover is that there is a real "paper tiger" at work in this facet of his sexism. He has the most trouble defending this aspect of his sexism, even to himself, and *it is by far the hardest for him to enforce.*

I think that politically, it's very important to agitate women to explore abandoning the shitwork, even in little "safe" ways because as they do it they will demonstrate to themselves in a most personal way, how weak the system is, how much it depends on women to enforce it. Young women are in the best position of all, as they can refuse to do it from the git go. Here, we do have "strike" power. But the difference is, we never, never go back to "work."

―❦―

What will this accomplish? We're still in the system. Nothing much has changed. Visibly. But in *the whole economy of human survival*, there takes place a great and potent shift of energy. This shift is (slowly) already underway as changing (formal) expectations of women have been achieved by rumors of women's liberation. It is now not only possible that men will do (a little) of their shitwork, but socially sanctioned.

I think that politically, we should pay more attention, agitate much more around this "trivia" (even at the expense of less attention to getting into "male" jobs), because potentially, it's far more revolutionary. It affects *all* women, whether they live with men or not and cumulatively, it liberates billions of hours of time into the power of women.

I've actually heard people argue that this could not have a revolutionary effect because women won't necessarily know "how" to use it. (This is like saying it's better not to give workers better wages. They'll just waste the money.) Women might just watch soap operas. Women are so uneducated they might just use it to rest. (God forbid). This reveals a misunderstanding of revolution. Billions of hours of accumulated energy (time) in the power of women would be used as women choose to use it, and women will define just what their interests are.

⁕

One of the "solutions" to the man question posed by the shitwork they create, a very popular one espoused often by socialists, is the creation of "shitwork industries." In a planned economy, not run for profit, laundries can be established so that people won't have to launder their own clothes; kitchens in or near the workplace can provide the major meals of the day. A great deal of shitwork can be eliminated simply by eliminating poverty itself.

True. And yet no economy in the world is going to allocate resources to build a robot which will pluck beard hairs out of the sink; wipe urine off of the walls and floors (Why can't they aim after lifetimes of practice?). Nobody will build Piss Palaces where men can shoot together in brotherhood over their own sticky floors. The dream of turning the shitwork over to some (future) state and converting it all into well-planned industries may have instances of validity, but is also informed with the persistent desire of men to avoid their own mess,

and a deep, abiding ignorance of the nature of shitwork itself, of what shitwork is, on the part of the gender which does not do it.

⁕

Some women are so justifiably outraged at all the shitwork they are forced to do, for free, all of their lives, for men, that they have organized great campaigns to get paid for it. But ultimately, the answer is for men to clean up after themselves.

This will only happen when they start cleaning up after children and taking responsibility for children. Children have to teach men about the real (human) nature of animal maintenance work, not women. Children recognize and can instruct men in the power and the paradox of human being.

Little children cherish their shit. They do not demean their animal selves. There is nothing inherently degrading about doing shitwork. On the contrary, it enhances our lives with the dignity of order and the fragrance of what is clean. It is men who degrade themselves by not doing their own shitwork, not women who are degraded because they do.

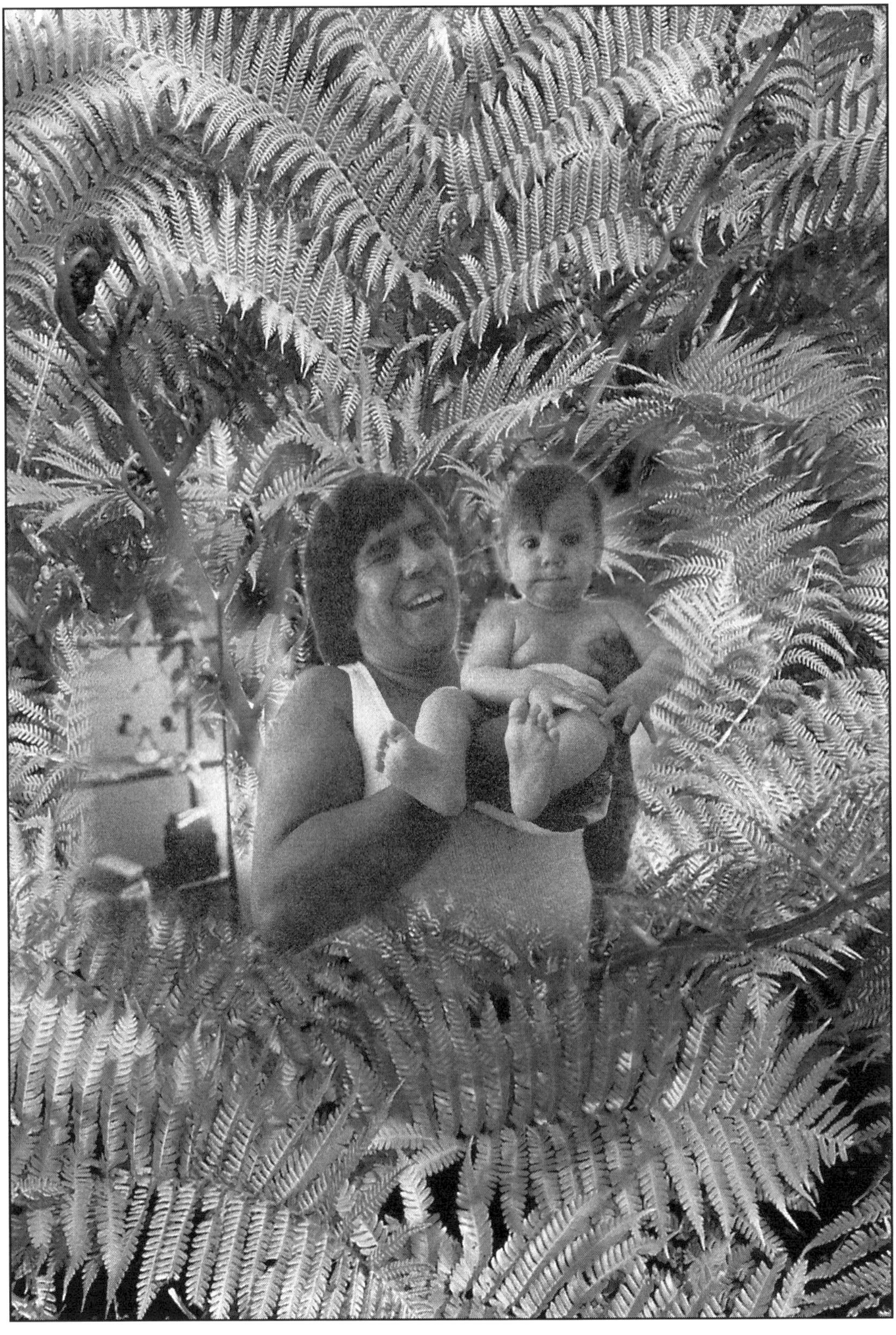

XI

A Vision

I offer a utopian vision because, although it may be not wholly achievable as I imagine it, it provides a target, something to aim for, a direction along which we can push our dreams as we build the road to them.

I envision a world in which all the labor necessary to human survival is shared equally by women and men.

Achieving such a world depends on our external struggle for political power over our lives and the internal struggles we have to wage for strength and self-esteem. Children are central to the vision, and so before it can be described, I would like to discuss the invisible axis around which change will turn, and this is: why people have children in the first place.

·⁐⁐·

We can discard physical instinct, at least as it has been understood up to the present. Looking beyond the myth of maternal instinct, it is clear that many children are born for lack of sex education, contraceptives, or availability of abortion. Some are born out of the social alienation of young women who have been unable to locate any other meaningful relationship. Others are born out of social pressure: many women are denied self-esteem in their cultures if they don't have children, are told that they are incomplete, violaters of nature if they don't have children. There are contexts in which men are pressured to impregnate women as proof of their masculinity.

In very poor countries, very poor people have many children and privileged people tell themselves that those who are poor do this to provide themselves "security" in their old age. Objectively, this seems absurd. Economically, the more children there are, the more the family is impoverished. As for emotional security, having many children in conditions of severe poverty is one factor leading to a guarantee of never even reaching old age. Something else very powerful seems to be going on. I lived in one of those countries for a long time and observed that apart from ignorance, apart from social pressure, apart from all notions of "macho," there is a certain defiance at work. Those people are not dumb. They can assess their location in the human order, the possibilities and limitations of their lives. What is going on is the human motivation for having children, which is as strong as the unconscious flow of reproduction in animals, but being human is more flexible, more accessible to control. They do it (apart from all other circumstance)

for the adventure.

Denied wealth, education, all but the most limited and unrewarding labor on the most infertile land or in the most tedious and insecure jobs, they cannot be denied this one great role—this one great, infinitely interesting and infinitely promising labor which is universally recognized as one of the greatest of all human adventures. Moreover, there is great reward in it, as all childworkers know. The reward is not economic, nor is it postponed to the end of life. The reward is self discovery, and it is born in the hunger for self esteem.

Bringing forth a child automatically confers a role of great importance on the parents. They become godlike in relation to someone else. They are challenged to fulfill this role. There is no other such challenge in the labor provided in conditions of poverty. The creation of a family is a personal one, a human drama in which to be human. In the creation of these human relations is sought the meaning of being human, of life itself. In family relations lie the riches of the poor. This is the labor into which their humanity is channeled.

In our families we can discover and develop our human beauty, even if every other channel of human development has been closed to us. Children infuse the work of the poor with a great self transcending meaning, make their lives and their struggles, precious.

Furthermore, people have so much to give, and there is no human order to receive these human gifts other than the one they have the power to create. This is true at the personal level, where families are made, and at the collective level, where they can create revolutions.

In developed capitalist countries where wealth is distributed (a little bit) more evenly than in the countries they colonize, and in countries with some socialist features in their economies such as Norway and Sweden where wealth is more evenly distributed, the birthrates are much lower than in poor countries. The more wealth is distributed, the lower the birthrate. This is even true within countries. The poor have more children than the rich.

In what we have come to call the developed world, a woman of (relative) privilege, education, perhaps of a feminist consciousness--a woman who knows, beyond the deadly, patriarchal, romantic myths, what children are, will often choose to have a child. Why?

For the adventure.

As things are now, the majority of the families of the world are based on heterosexual unions, on a nuclear family which is more or less extended according to the norms and economies of different cultures. I would like to project a future in which the families in which we live are far more extended than those I know; housing built for them so that the life of a child (so that everyone's life) would organically encounter and transact energies with the aged, with both sexes on many points of the life continuum—at the daily level, where it counts.

Be that as it may evolve, we can speculate with some security that when the revolution succeeds and we take power over our lives, it is likely to be in a situation in which the majority of families of the world are based on heterosexual unions, on a nuclear family more or less extended. I don't see anything wrong with this. Many feminists would like to believe that families as we form them now are to blame for our personal ills—that some radical restructuring of the family will have to take place before we can rescue our personal lives from patriarchy.

From the Marxist point of view, this implies another ten thousand years of change (it will take a long, long time). And many feminists go careening off into visions of "collectives" where the children are somehow raised by "everybody." In these visions, people come floating in and out of sexual relationships with each other and parent relationships with children in a kind of theater lobby fluidity with which one would buy or discard a bag of popcorn. Children who were unhappy with one or another floating "parent" could "choose" another (This would be hilarious at age two). All such visions are kind of hilarious unless you look at it with a child's eyes. From a child's point of view, it is harrowing. But the idea that structural change in the family is somehow going to need another ten millennia or so to "work itself out" is dangerous. That is patriarchy speaking, not "human nature."

·⁂·

Under conditions of substantial gender equality, the union of a woman and a man will not (re)produce the poisoned relationships of the past. It isn't the union or parenting of a woman and a man which make the conditions of family life so oppressive. It's the conditions of poverty, the inequality of the genders, and the lack (among heterosexual couples) of shared parenting.

Many people who are justifiably horrified by present family relations are queasy about the "ego" relationship they perceive parents have in relation to their children; see that parents may seek not only self-discovery, but self-reproduction in their children—that there are parents who wish to turn out little replicas of themselves or turn children into their (unfulfilled) dreams.

Under present conditions of ignorance, frustration, and inequality, these ideas do sometimes contaminate the parenting of some people, in different degrees. Under patriarchy they always have. But I don't think we need to be so afraid of this. All too often these fears are informed by woman hatred (got to get rid of those all-powerful devouring FEMALE (mothers)

and they are deeply informed by the patriarchal conditioning we have all had smashed into our brains from infancy that human nature, especially as it is expressed between men and women, is exploitative, power hungry, and sick. Patriarchy would have us believe that we are all or all would like to be patriarchs. If this were the case, the "solution" would have to take the form of separating children off from their parents as much as possible, meaning that

individual human unions cannot be trusted with children.

Biological mothers cannot be trusted.

Men cannot be trusted.

So who can be trusted?

The state, say the Marxists.

Anarchy, say (a few) feminists.

It gets silly. I think that under conditions of gender equality (not just economic equality as it is conceived of by Marxists), family relations will be detoxified by the fresh air of dignity.

Having children is, under the best of circumstances, and must remain, a personal decision. And the personal adventure sought in the creation of children under conditions of gender equality can be fulfilled so that the lives of parents and children are mutually fulfilling beyond any relations we have ever known in the fetid chambers of male dominated patriarchal family life in which men do not share equal responsibility for primary childwork with women.

Just as you can recognize racism, every time, in any argument which relinquishes responsibility for racism against people of color on the part of any white person in our society, or tries to fob it off on other white persons, you can recognize patriarchy, every time, in any argument which relinquishes the responsibility for primary childwork to women, or tries to fob it off on some special *group* of women. These oppressions are not the same, but some of the mechanisms are the same.

~·~

Depersonalizing childwork is a terrible loss to all who bear children as well as to the children themselves. The personal involvement of childworkers with the children is of immense importance to both. I don't see anything "wrong" with the pride people feel in their children. It is an objective fact that no one is as passionately interested in an individual child as that child's parents. No amount of rhetoric will ever change it, nor should it be changed. There is nothing wrong with this personal passion. On the contrary, it is a deep and irreplaceable source of self esteem for a child, and a source of adult commitment making accessible to a child the deepest levels of us. It is the territory of the adventure.

Fears of "ego" involvement are not only based on patriarchal definitions of what humans are, but are silly on their own terms. In fact, parents never do succeed in cloning themselves and children never do fulfill their parents' personal dreams. In fact, most parents, especially women, who do most of the real parenting, make superhuman efforts to do well by their children. And in the context of all the racist, capitalist, patriarchal obstacles confronting these efforts, succeed (and this is a great wonder) in preserving in both their children's lives and their own some degree of dignity and love. Often, great degrees of both. People can be trusted with their children.

~·~

Depersonalizing childwork is a terrible loss to a child. The daily idiosyncrasies, the body of shared personal experience which accumulate over years of personal interaction between a child and a childworker constitute the very solid ground of uninterrupted, psychic comparison, the deep human continuity and sense of security by which each new experience may be safely, insightfully, calibrated.

Depersonalizing childwork is a terrible loss to the adults who sought the adventure of children, and who need the socialization that only children can provide.

Depersonalizing childwork is a great loss to society. Children are not auto bodies. Childwork is not performed in a capital goods manufacturing plant subject to industrial management. If the personal adventure is taken out of it, humans are not motivated to have children.

For men to share childwork equally with women, we will have to begin creating some social machinery which does not now exist.

One thing we could do is create centers which would revolve around childwork. These would be places which would enable children to socialize both men and women into new relations.

Men (and women as well) would meet the challenges of childwork in physical and psychological conditions far superior to those that women experienced in the past.

・༺༻・

We know now that the human brain is remarkably plastic, not only in childhood, but throughout human adulthood as well. The brain restructures itself and its activities in response to environmental challenges with great dexterity. The brains of men doing childwork would reflect their engagement, just as do the minds of women doing childwork.

Sociality affects the brain and the body in many dimensions, including cardiovascular activity, hormone production and distribution, the pleasure/reward system, immune function, and regulation of aggression.

We also know that in mammal species in which the effects of male parenting have been studied, males who participate significantly in caring for their young accrue the same kind of cognitive benefits which have been shown to result from motherhood in the females, and that oxytocin plays a significant role in male parenting. Also among humans, near the end of a pregnancy, the body of the male partner produces high levels of a hormone found in lactating women, prolactin. Cuddling his baby, smelling the baby's vernix, decreases testosterone, and increases prolactin and cortisol.

When men live close to their babies and children,

their psyches will inevitably conform

to the contours

of the neurobiological substrates of love

elicited and shaped by the children.

This experience will color the psyches of men in ways distinct to men, but recognizable to women.

Animal studies are revealing that, triggered by the environment, great changes can take place from one generation to the next through epigenetics; that we don't need to wait for the slow unfolding of evolutionary changes exclusive to our genes.

We are in control of our future selves.

·～·

In some countries, at the present time, women get one year of maternity leave. As a beginning, we could start out with a demand for a two year leave, for both parents. Prior to birth, both parents (heterosexual or otherwise) would be required to attend birthing/new child classes where they would come into contact with other parents preparing for the adventure. After the birth of a child, the exhausting demands of a newborn would be split equally between the parents twenty-four hours a day. No woman or man would be introduced to their child through the exhausting ordeal of prolonged sleep deprivation. If a woman is breastfeeding a child every two to four hours, twenty-four hours a day, she would barely need be woke, if she were sleeping, half of the time, because for half of the time it would be a father who heeds the baby's cry, changes it, delivers it to the breast, returns it to crib or cradle. Here I envision that men

> will watch
>
> in the silence of the night
>
> the ecstatic motion
>
> of the fingers and hands of an infant
>
> at breast
>
> men whose thoughts,
>
> souls
>
> may drift unimpeded in the incense of vernix
>
> men, too, who modulate
>
> their low voices

into lulling songs of love.

(these songs will emerge from men

who have never sung before

just as they emerge from women

who have never before sung)

The passion inspired

by this ecstasy of trust

is as deep and rhythmic as sex.

Infants will hear the human heart

beating in the muscular breasts of men

gaze raptly

into the eyes of men.

Men, too will learn the exquisite sensuality

of manipulating the silken bodies of babies

into and out of garments, water, embrace;

be startled,

in the first days and months,

by strange sputterings

as the nervous system kicks into gear

and learn

of what they are made.

Men

who will enter into the unselfconscious gaze of infants

and explore

the exquisite purity of an unconditioned

human consciousness;

meet wonder

timelessness

the pristine contours of an unknown infinity,

all of the things

men are looking for in outer space.

Men will have time to surrender

to the fascination

of watching babies.

Little babies are as seductive of the unconscious

as relaxing

and subversive of the human ego

as fire

as surf.

This brief period, between birth and toddlerhood,

is the only window we are ever offered

onto

fully revealed

humanity.

Men will observe and measure the number of changes in facial expression flickering across the face of a baby in one minute, explode this logrithmically across a day

and learn

how much we mask.

Men in whom will emerge

a sense,

over the days, months, and years

of the rhythm of human development

surging

in diurnal, mensual, yearly waves;

feel these rhythms

manipulating their labor

feel these rhythms move their own bodies

their own minds

and learn

what is truly

potent.

Men whose senses will be flooded with delight

at the sound of a burp

who will anticipate with tender solidarity

the release of the recalcitrant stool

who will learn to respect

and cherish

the human body: understand the human meaning

the human need

the human love

in cleanliness.

Men who will be reborn in their adulthood

through all the "firsts"

the first contact with grass

with sand

with wind.

The first, orgiastic encounter with a

ripe strawberry.

The first, mind-boggling confrontation

with another species.

Men will learn at last what is going on between

all those numinous madonnas

and awestruck babies

gazing at each other with those zonko expressions

will stumble astonished

into a precipitous

lifelong

love affair

with a stranger.

Men

will finally learn

about life.

Men will see themselves

and their labor

mirrored in the undistorted purity

of a child's consciousness

of a child's reactions

of a child's wellbeing.

For children *do* reflect us:

They reflect our labor.

Not our ideas,

but our labor.

Men will

find themselves

in children.

And the priorities of men

will finally become

the real

(and not imagined)

priorities of children.

Men will be rewarded for this labor

by the love of children,

love informed with the passion until now reserved

for the mother.

(Men will learn what passion is).

Men will be rewarded for this labor

by the love of women

who share this adventure with them

and who have always longed to share this adventure with them

but who have been ignored and isolated in it

for millenia.

Men will be rewarded for this labor

by the love of other men

with whom they will share

at last

a labor which unites them

not in the fear and contempt of women

but in the concrete love of children.

Men will be rewarded in this labor

by self love.

I don't envision those two years as two years of isolation, excluding any other kind of work,

   but the primary childwork

   must be divided between the parents.

A social organization for childworkers would facilitate discussion, problem solving, and expression of ideas about the work with other couples. The unit of organization most organic might be a group from a given neighborhood, district, or rural region, which would meet, soon after the notification of a positive result in a pregnancy test in the case of a wanted child.

In the process of applying for prenatal care/education, the partners would be assigned to a birthing class comprised of all the couples who were going to give birth in a given set of months in a given region (district, neighborhood). That group would be their childwork organization which would meet at a local childwork center. Such centers could be built by the government or, during the transitional stage, existing facilities could be designated and turned over to the parents of a given area.

The couple would go to this center for childbirth classes and be instructed in early prenatal and postnatal childwork, meet and interact with other new childworkers preparing for the adventure.

After the birth of a child, and during the next two years, parents would be required to go to their childwork center and take courses on first aid and human development. This would keep them in contact with parents like themselves and they could share the discoveries and the tips their labor would generate.

Such childwork facilities could have rooms in them designed for infants and early toddlers, where parents could safely put them down on the floor and interact with one another in the presence of their children, and watch other people's babies, too. They could have rooms where one or another parent not on duty at the moment could shoot pool, read, have political discussions, or just relax and socialize with other childworkers, male or female, away from coworkers and children.

Centers could have nurseries open where fulltime professional childworkers relieve the parents of primary work to enjoy activities together away from child(ren). All childworkers could be issued tokens of so many hours a week of this service and redeem them as they chose. Parents would have access to these facilities and could alternate childwork between the quiet convenience of their homes and the social atmosphere of the center with its many toys and child and adult activities, around the schedule and idiosyncrasies of any individual child at any state of development.

   What's being described here are

GOOD WORKING CONDITIONS.

·⸙·

The implacable democracy of assigning together as a group individual couples who become pregnant at any given time would automatically bring together people in given communities and unite their most disparate elements in common concrete labor. Society would probably learn more about itself in a childwork center than any university has ever taught.

·⸙·

I know that such a commitment of time to children isn't "necessary." Women alone can take one year of maternity leave and pay the price for one year of the adventure in twenty-four hour a day exhausting isolation. (And women even choose to. Given no other alternative, they willingly do this, so wonderful is this love affair, even under these discouraging conditions. Men should pay attention to this.)

Women alone can do it, and after one year, while the child is still a baby, a woman can indeed rip herself away from her baby. There is a real trauma in this, for both. This trauma has acquired social respectability in modern patriarchal societies. Women are told that this wrenching pain is "guilt" and made to feel ashamed of it, asked to hide it, even from themselves. This is not "guilt," but longing. Babies are not propagandized into any sort of "explanation" for *their* grief.

Babies can be lined up on cots for their naps, assembly line fed, bathed, and diapered. This can be done quite efficiently in an atmosphere of benevolent, depersonalized, patriarchal care by women who are truly interested in their welfare

> but not passionately involved with any one of them
>
> and who have no time to allow a bath
>
> to explode into a big, prolonged personal, joyful adventure;
>
> who have no time
>
> to surrender to anybody's fertile anarchy
>
> when it's time now to round them up and feed them.

This can be done.

The children do not "die."

The mother of the child can go about her other work

loaded with the ambivalence of pain and duty

throughout the elapsing hours of the babyhood

of her absent baby.

It isn't "necessary" to personalize childwork, even for one year.

Infants can be lined up, held at intervals, and serviced. This "liberates" the mothers into "productive" labor. We must ask ourselves what we most want our society to produce. We need to recognize that this so-called "liberation" of mothers entails the complete waste of the labor of children. The labor of children is to give birth to us.

The two years following birth are the best years for the adventure to be shared by men and women, full time, because it is during those two years that children most need us, are the most helpless. I can anticipate the horror of men at the thought of "wasting" the labor of not only a woman, but an able-bodied man (!) for two years. Women have always done it alone. It can't require that much time and labor to "care" for a baby. And it doesn't. They can be "cared" for in nurseries, for that matter.

But women haven't been just "caring" for babies

like men "care" for cattle

all these long millenia.

Women have been childworking them

and childwork is labor

and love

intensive.

Women have also been exhausted.

It is a male idea that a woman

doesn't have much to do

"except"

"take care" of the baby

in addition to whatever else she does.

It is true that women in preindustrial economies strap the baby on and toil in the fields. Women in preindustrial economies have no choice. Their lifespans are not very long and their babies suffer a high mortality rate as well. Poor women in both industrial and preindustrial economies often leave the babies with the aged women of those economies. The new economy we establish must not be permitted to exploit older women in that way.

And it's true that women can be found (and photographed) who have "raised" three children, served in an important community post, kept spotless homes, achieved recognition and success in their (paid) jobs, jog five miles a day, whose husbands think they are the bee's knees.

These women are dressed impeccably, are trim, and have dazzling smiles.

We all know these women.

We meet them, day after day, in the pages of *Cosmopolitan*; *Ebony*; *Parent's Magazine*

on the TV shows

There must be hordes of them clamoring for interviews on the local 'Lifestyle' pages

because the *Parade* never ends.

I've never met one. I've never met any woman who does half of that who is not either

neurotic

exhausted

taking speed

or some combination thereof.

I've never met one

but I know them well.

They are as familiar as liquor ads.

I don't want to demean the lives and labor of many, many women who have done truly superhuman work, on all fronts, always. We all know the human spirit overcomes oppression. We all know that the oppressed are superproductive. But babies are a twenty-four hour a day shift, and splitting that shift between two workers is not an unreasonable division of labor.

The two years following birth are ideal for personalized childwork also because that's about the maximum before children develop a full set of teeth and most women lose interest in breastfeeding, if they didn't lose interest before.

Masturbating one's milk off into sterile bottles and refrigerating it so that you can go back to important "work" is just not the same as breastfeeding a child and few women do it for long, if they can bring themselves to do it at all.

Those two years are ideal for both parents to be fully involved in a child because those are the years when children are indiscriminate enough to value adults as much as adults value them. After two years, language and and ego (selfconsciousness) blossom out.

After the first twelve months, when children graduate from infancy and become mobile, social interaction with their peers begins to take on more significance. Parents can continue to meet in the childwork center in free social interaction with themselves and their children for classes, but now there can be regular playgroups of children where parents take their children for the better part of an afternoon or a morning. All parents would be personally responsible for their children during playgroup and present at them (perhaps alternating a different partner each day). Children are still too young to organize on their own into games, dance, and song at this time, but can be gently guided into these social activities by participating parents

and enjoy them

and enjoy each other under those circumstances, very much.

This is the beginning of full socialization and the beginning of the separation between child and childworker. At eighteen, twenty, twenty-two months, children can begin to be left by their parents in the childwork center for an hour, two hours, then for a few hours at a time.

Any professional childwork, from nurseries through playgroups through fulltime schedules, would need to be staffed equally by well-paid males and females. At two years of age, the child could be ushered into loosely structured play and education with peers, supervised by professional childworkers half days. Both parents could return to other work part-time. Two-year-olds still require exhausting childwork that would be split evenly between the parents.

When the child reaches three years of age, the parents return to their regular work schedules. At three, children are articulate and vitally interested in their independent lives. Under these conditions, they will be emotionally secure.

At three years of age, they are also

gendered.

The adults who return to work would be educated. They could bring back to their jobs human insight never before integrated into the entire labor of a society. These are the workers a healthy society should seek to produce, and only children can produce them.

Of course, the adventure doesn't end there, but before describing this proposal further, or speculating about the mechanisms by which such a human organization could be reinforced, I want to emphasize that it is not the family which we need to restructure. It is our labor which must be restructured to achieve our human liberation. An economy which would make this possible would have to be restructured, at first, around many dislocations. The way we rear and gender ourselves is only one part of a vision of a better world. The world we want to build will require building new housing, hospitals, and schools while salvaging and improving existing ones. We will have to clean up the environment, demobilize armies, destroy and recycle millions of tons of military garbage, rip up thousands upon thousands of square miles of asphalt suffocating precious, fertile earth, build mass transit systems.

There won't be enough jackhammers.

We'll have to put the jackhammer factories on doubletime.

I can hear the thuds and the crashing and the teethrattling racket of the chompgnashing jackhammers

as they free the earth from her prison.

She is going to forgive.

She is going to give us fruits and flowers.

It is going to be an emerge

ency.

For the first time we can create a society not built on the backs of the unpaid and unreciprocated labor of a socially demeaned gender.

◦⌒⌒⌒◦

When I say we have to restructure our labor, I mean we have to restructure it for the liberation of children, not only of women and men. Children must be allowed the right of self-discovery, the rewards of self-esteem brought by real work in the social relations of production. Children can be given, not only crayons and throw-away paper, but real paint and real tools and real training in the properties of concrete, stucco, wood and plaster, and set to decorating all the walls and all the halls of our now grim hospitals, offices, prisons, and other human environs.

Children can be given, not only plastic pretend tools but real tools, spades and hoes and hoses and rakes and set to planting the new parks the jackhammers have liberated from the parking lots.

Real parks, where they relate to the tree they planted twenty years later, not just the fragmentary memory of an avocado pit in a paper cup someone mysteriously discards.

Childworkers can take children to clean the beaches, clean and maintain parks and public spaces in neighborhoods.

The centers can organize vacation camps where whole families can re(create), dedicating half their days to unstructured lolling around and the other half to reforestation.

I'm not suggesting that we should put the children to (our version of) work fulltime. Only that, according to their ages, all children should have some concrete daily responsibility in the development and maintenance of the world all humans live in; that the society we want is not going to be a world we are forced to constantly "protect" them from; that children are not helpless and never have been. We must begin showing respect for children, respect for their labor.

Children can produce plays and songs to perform for construction workers, for patients in hospitals, for offices, mines, factories, laboratories. Children should be allowed into all the places to sing and smirk. They should be afforded every possibility of making themselves heard in our workplaces, their art in front of us, everywhere, not wadded up and disposed of after a hypocritical display of "appreciation."

Older children can be taught about younger children; class time structured so they have some "class" in which they have some responsibility toward the younger ones. They can learn, in a childwork center, for example, to bathe the little ones; groom them, even just be given a fifteen minute assignment to see if they can elicit laughter from the littler ones.

I'm talking about integration.

Throughout the years of the adventure, parents would be required to continue their education in human development, and take those classes in the childwork center. The center would continue to provide parents with tokens to be redeemed for safe, competent childwork to relieve them of primary responsibility so that they could enjoy free time away from children.

All parents would have responsibilities to serve the childwork center itself, so many hours a month, doing cooking, cleaning, administrative chores or whatever was needed: gender integrated obligations. All parents would be required to meet in their center at regular intervals during their child's growing years. Not voluntary PTA meetings, but mandatory childwork center meetings. All problems and innovations regarding childwork, and the education of children and their workers could be discussed in such meetings. Part of meetings would be set aside for self-governance.

At the outset you might ask, well if everybody got a two year leave, what would keep people from having a lot of babies?

Nothing would keep people from having a lot of babies if that was truly what they wanted to do, but if gender integration is enforced, I don't think the system would be abused, because babies are a lot of work and each additional baby would be that much more work. If the work is really being done (if the children are not neglected), and if the work is truly gender integrated, nobody is going to be having a vacation. After one or two or three children, the burdens of the work itself militate against having a baby for the sake of two years away from another job. Children are a lot of work and children are not the whole adventure, are not enough, as women know. In such a society there would be alternatives. There would be much more to refresh women's lives than another new baby.

I think it is socially enforceable, and in a much more humane way, for everybody involved, than the way childwork is exclusively forced on women at the present time. Marriage contracts can make both parties legally responsible for one half of all childwork for any child issuing from the marriage. Assignment of parents to a childwork center, attendance at classes and meetings would be compulsory for both parents.

Within the home, the equal division of childwork and attendant shitwork would be left to the discretion of the coworkers. If one of them (and here we are all imagining the woman) feels that the other is not sharing the work equitably, that person could take the grievance to a meeting. The members of the group can hear both sides and come to some decision about it in favor of one party or the other, and offer support to both. If the conflict were not resolved there, the childwork center would be a place to provide family counselors to work more intensively with the couple. These counselors would be trained in humanistic, feminist principles of sociology and psychology. If the offensive behavior of one of the parties continued through all that, the childwork group, or the counselor, or both, would have to refer the case to the justice system outside of the childwork center. Child neglect and spousal abuse are serious crimes.

In practice, men who actually engage in serious childwork prove to be good at it, proud of it, and are apt to judge men who goof off severely, especially since they themselves are making serious efforts to do it well and will have real feeling for children.

In practice, all these people would come to know each other and know that they will know each other for a long time, and will seek each other's esteem. Women would no longer be powerless in the face of male irresponsibility. Just the idea of having selfish behavior aired before a meeting would be inhibiting.

Legal reinforcements would have to be created, but in practice, in the great majority of the cases, childwork would be enforced on men by the real power which has always enforced it on women, and that is, children.

If we institute such social organizations or something similar to them, I think that once men are integrated with children, the children will seduce them. The children will take power over them, over their minds, their imaginations, their hearts, their labor, just as they have always taken power over us, in the wake of our forced integration with children.

·⁂·

Women might be afraid that this would mean that they wouldn't find marriage partners, but I don't think that needs to be a central worry. Most men and most women, both heterosexual and homosexual, look, eventually, for stable unions, and they do this not only in response to social pressure, but out of human need. Adults need stable unions as badly as children do. Family is a need.

Another mechanism at work in favor of male acceptance of this arrangement is that men will not be united against it. Even now there are men who would welcome the chance to share childwork; who are fighting for "paternity" leaves; whose silouettes can be seen, here and there, at rallies, on buses, with a big bump on their fronts or on their backs. Even now there are men who seriously question the brutal macho ethos they are supposed to enforce on each other; men propagandizing against violence toward women; men offering counseling to other men who beat women.

We already have male allies.

I think what would happen is that men who desire (real) children, men who seek real community with women,

will be the most desirable men around.

Such men will be the focus of female attention, female desire. Those will be the men women seek to love. And we all know that macho posturing is not enough. That when it comes to the real evaluation, heterosexual men measure their masculinity, and each other's masculinity, in part, by the power they exercise over women, their power to attract women. The bozos will be left behind.

Many men who are not enthusiastic about such a plan will go along with it just so that they won't "look" bad, to women, or to themselves, or the society. That's OK. Once obligated to put themselves in the range of the power of children, children will take power over them and they will not regret their willingness to enter such relations.

The children can be trusted with the men.

Meanwhile, a new "norm" would be building up—a new institution which would take on all the normalcy and self-regenerative power of other social institutions:

the equal sharing of all the labor necessary to human survival and development by women and men.

Any other arrangement will come to be, come to "feel" alien.

·⌒⌒·

I can imagine, too, a form of legal reinforcement consisting of a requirement that people holding any "leadership" positions in government would have to have either childworked one of his or her own children in order to be eligible, or to have served two consecutive years of fulltime childwork (involving significant training) to even qualify for nomination to such positions.

The people who don't want children (either biological or adopted), could fulfill this obligation in a childwork center. The obligation wouldn't be forced on anyone. People who totally rejected any personal responsibility for (real children) would be free to do so all of their lives. But they would not be allowed positions of leadership in any domain of human life affecting children or children's future.

No longer would we be subject to the outrageous arrogance of government officials mouthing off in "the interest of our nation's youth" and the "future of society," who did not have any real experience or real interest in "the nation's youth," vomit and tears and all, and the credentials (with a good record on those credentials) to prove it. It would mean not having to tolerate male politicians invoke their "fatherhood," who posture in front of TV cameras with "I am a father myself," and "My wife and I have two children," and "...the world we want our children to live in," and "I have two kids myself..."

Who is he kidding?

Where's the kid?

His wife

"has" the kid.

Men think their penises give them power.

Power comes from labor.

No one will be given power over the future of humans who has not labored with the human future of society.

Women have already earned the first priority in determining that future. There's no reason for any timidity on our part in demanding these changes, or changes like them. We have already earned the right to determine the designs of childwork with thousands upon thousands of years of unpaid, unreciprocated, unappreciated, unrecognized, unremitting

LABOR

not "caring."

One consequence of such a social order would be to eliminate at last the built-in advantage which men exercise against any possibility of women's concrete empowerment to take advantage of the "opportunities" so hypocritically offered them for "leadership" in patriarchal societies. Everyone knows, lip service be damned, that withdrawing from the job, interrupting the development of a career, in any industry or government is (under present conditions), a "backward" step. You get taken out of circulation.

Men in patriarchal societies who aspire to leadership very effectively winnow out all but token female "leadership" because the majority of women succumb, sooner or later, to their human desire to have children, and never "catch up." The way things really work, whether in the local philatelic society, on the job, or in a political party, is that the people who take on the most work are those most prepared to be leaders. If the two genders are not equally available for such work, then the gender which *is* available, gets it.

Without a universal demand for childwork credentials for leadership, there is a built in mechanism eliminating from leadership people who love and desire (real) children. If credentials are required, everybody will be equally "handicapped" and children will be afforded the opportunity to exercise their power, to some extent at least, over every single human being at every level of society who influences their lives or pretends to speak in their interest.

It would be a society that does not just *claim* that children are its first priority, *claims* that it intends to give children more than material security, lip service, and gussied up ghettoes.

It would be a society intending to give children power,

to give

itself

to children.

Does anybody care about what the children want?

That's what they want.

You can put a little child and his or her childworker in a room full of glittering toys and what the child will go for, every time, is the attention of and interaction with the childworker. Privileged people learn this quickly. You can't buy your way out of their demanding interest. No toy does it. No plush rooms do it.

Many poor people know this. They know that the happiness of children, beyond the most basic fulfillment of their biological needs, depends on our giving of ourselves to them. That's what children want. Us.

⁂

Perhaps in the transitional stage, economic incentives (as understood by the former society) would still be useful and necessary. Professional childworkers would receive the highest pay of all workers in society. They would get the most benefits and the best housing. They would be the most extensively and intensively educated. They would belong to their own union and have voice and vote at the highest levels of our political order.

This would be, not only a reversal of the patriarchal order wherein childwork is the lowest paid and considered, in typical patriarchal fashion, "dead" "end" (when it is really the life end—patriarchy doesn't know its ass from its brain), but will also accelerate gender integration in childwork among men who are still conditioned to equate material success with their fulfillment.

The self esteem so generated among childworkers won't go unrecorded in the minds of the children they childwork.

⁂

I believe that this arrangement I envision or something similar to it would resolve a number of contradictions which presently crush childworkers and children. It would make it possible to reap the rewards of childwork as a personal adventure, while going much further toward protecting children from personal abuse than has ever been possible under any economic system. All children and their childworkers would be visible to the rest of society. The process would be intimate and personal, but not so private that abuse toward children could go unperceived by many adults, not just one or a few. Moreover, it would be perceived by adults who had the power to do something about it.

No man could sexually abuse a child without being exposed publicly. No woman would be helpless to protect her child from such abuse. It would not be easy for a woman or a man to be addicted to alcohol and abuse children unseen either by a partner or the public. Concrete remedial action could be undertaken, swiftly. Not action relegated to the isolated coworker, but action taken, swiftly, by the whole society in an organization devoted to children's interests, not as a peripheral annoyance laden with patriarchal definitions which reduce children to private property, but as a primary concern and a primary responsibility.

Childworkers could enjoy this wonderful personal adventure, and still be held accountable for the responsible exercise of the right to do so.

It is even possible that the social ties created by this arrangement or something similar to it could provide a middle ground between our longing for a place in an extended family—formerly, and in many places still, a tribe—and our alienation in the relatively isolated positions we occupy in modern industrial societies.

Childwork under such conditions would be much different than it is now. Just taking the exhaustion out of it would revolutionize the experience of both worker and child. Conflicts between child and childworker could be quantitatively reduced, making childhood itself a qualitatively different experience, for every human.

Men need not fear the horrors of the experience that they observe in it today. Childwork will not entail suffering, self-abnegation, isolation, loss of prestige, poisonous dependencies, or contempt, because childworkers will no longer be exploited.

Men will never know what we have suffered and will never have to undergo what we have undergone. Men will be free to take the adventure and bring to it their minds, their human power, creative abilities, insights

most fruitfully

and birth themselves.

This power to birth themselves is what men have been seeking all along.

The world in which we have to try to implement this continues and will continue to be full of imbalances. There would be many single mothers, for instance. We will have to have provisional arrangements exposing children and men to one another, in the workplace, through the establishment of childwork credentials for leadership, aggressive recruitment of men for high paid labor in childwork centers, perhaps even voluntary labor on the part of our allies, while the system kicks in.

Now imagine that in eighteen years the children of the provisional arrangements would come into their majority and every successive year, children would emerge out of a childwork system progressively more gender integrated.

How many generations would it take to eliminate patriarchy altogether? If "generation" is taken to mean the average span of time between the birth of parents and that of their offspring, and the "parents" are reckoned to be the first youth to have spent their entire childhood in the new system, beginning in the transitional period with provisional arrangements, I think it might only take three generations to eliminate patriarchy. Somewhere between sixty and eighty years. About the lifetime of a human.

It could be the shortest revolution on record.

It doesn't matter about men's "attitudes" during the transition. Men could talk about their maleness, could consciously even tell the little boys they are childworking about the need to be "macho"; remind the little girls how pretty they are, and so on. It isn't our ideas that most deeply influence children, it's what we do. The men could talk all they liked. What the kids would perceive is that machos change diapers; hold them when they cry; that machos don't get any more economic reward, prestige, or emotional support in life than women.

Envision a world in which all the former conditioning of men would be rendered empty posturing because these "attitudes" would be undermined by what really talks, their labor. All their "privileges,"

   the "privilege" of exercising violence against women and children

   the "privilege" of ignoring the lives of women and children

   of earning more than we do at our expense (for every man who has nothing, there is a woman who has less than nothing)

   the "privilege" of their fat leisure hours while we work

   the "privilege" of tyrannizing us (and I don't care how "benevolently" they exercise that tyranny) will shrivel and die, a ghastly echo, as remote as the screams of the trembling children stabbed, their living hearts symbolically or literally cut out to feed the egos of patriarchal males from Abraham to the altars of the Aztecs

for this is the meaning of patriarchy

the human sacrifice of children

the denial (erasure; murder) of children

by their fathers.

Only peripherally are the women sacrificed. Children are the targets of the sacrificial knives.

Every broken beer bottle shoved into our vaginas

every bayonet

every penis rapedaggered into our bodies

is aimed at the womb.

We are peripheral to the hatred of the patriarchs.

If we would only distance ourselves from the children

if only we would deny them, too

(murder them; erase them from our sight; reject personal involvement with them)

men will welcome us

into their society; give us money, leadership, respect.

Patriarchy is another word for hate

hate for the children

with whom we fall in love

and patriarchy can be defeated.

It is weak and empty.

It has no heart

no guts.

We have for too long bent over our babies, bloodied in fear.

It is nothing.

Strip off the mask of the high priest,

and you will find only the unborn.

·❦·

How can we make this vision a reality? We have colluded with patriarchy for thousands of years, given it "protection" money, tried to pay it off with fear. After epochs of such collaboration, there's no way to walk away from it without a fight. We have to include work for this vision with all the existing struggles for human justice—the struggles to restrain unfettered capitalism, to defeat racism. It is in these struggles where male dominance is the most incoherent, weakest, where it can be most readily challenged. These are the struggles, collectively undertaken, that lead to the better world we want.

We have to work in these struggles because it is absolutely in our interest to end unrestrained capitalism as we know it, which pays us 79 cents to the dollar for the work it pays us for at all, and buries us in toxic waste; to end imperialism which has irradiated our Micronesian sisters who now birth deformed life, who now weep in what must be the keenest agony ever reserved for women; to end racism which pits us and our children against each other.

Another reason is that this work is where the best men are to be found. The only men worth fighting for. The only men worth fighting with. And I do mean "fighting with" in both full senses of the fight. A better world can't be won without us. We can't huddle together outside of political struggles in contempt of the males who presently dominate them or stand outside jeering at those males for their confusion in matters of gender.

Men have been confused for a long time.

We, too, have been confused for a long time.

We are the majority. Even if the men are confused, we no longer need to be confused, cowed into "deferring" our struggle as if it were some task unrelated to the rest of human progress. There's no reason to respect the fear of men. Nor is there much time left before the machinery of the past comes to rest on its own logic, and engulfs us in environmental catastrophe. Our freedom has to be conceived in unity with men, whether they like it or not.

Once the children exercise power over the men, men will be our equals.

Power to the children.

I offer these thoughts to you hoping you'll take what is true to you, what may be needed or useful, and discard what is not, or hold it for further consideration, as events over time will prove or disprove. I don't expect you to "become" a revolutionary. You already are one. Anybody who can wake in the crib every morning at first light

and sing

is a revolutionary.

It is you who have taught me these things

you who have given me this vision

you seeking power over me, over your world,

over yourself

you singing away in your crib at dawn

who awakened me.

With abiding love,

Your mother.

References

Angelou, Maya. 1997. *The Heart of a Woman*. New York: Bantam Books.

Bingham, Sally. 1972. *The Way it is Now: Stories*. New York: Viking Press.

Caudwell, Christopher. 1946. *Illusion and Reality: A Study of the Sources of Poetry*. New York: International Publishers.

Chodorow, Nancy. 1978. *The Reproduction of Mothering: Psychoanalysis and the Sociology of Gender*. Berkeley, CA: University of California Press.

Dawkins, Richard. 1989. *The Selfish Gene*. Oxford University Press.

Dinnerstein, Dorothy. 1976. *The Mermaid and the Minotaur*. New York: Harper Colophon (1977 Paperback).

El Saadawi, Nawal. 1980. *The Hidden Face of Eve*. London: Zed Books Ltd.

Engels, Friedrich. 1880. Socialism: Utopian and Scientific. In: *Marx/Engels Selected Works, Volume 3*. Progress Publishers, 1970.

_____. 1884. Origins of the Family, Private Property, and the State. In: *Marx/Engels Selected Works, Volume 3*. Progress Publishers, 1974.

Firestone, Shulamith. 1970. *The Dialectic of Sex: The Case for Feminist Revolution*. New York: Bantam Books.

Folbre, Nancy. 2001. The Economy Sucks: Why Should Virtue be its own Reward? *Women's Review of Books*, July. 11-12.

Harding, Sandra. 1981. What is the Real Material Base of Patriarchy and Capital? In Lydia Sargent (Ed.) *Women and Revolution: A Discussion of the Unhappy Marriage of Marxism and Feminism*, Boston, MA: Southend Press. 135-163.

Hitler, Adolf. quoted in De Grazia, Alfred. 1952. *The Elements of Political Science*. Knopf, 1952. 556.

hooks, bell. 1981. *Ain't I a Woman: black women and feminism*. Boston, MA: South End Press.

Lenin, Vladimir I. 1920. On International Women's Day. In: *Women and Communism*. London: Lawrence & Wishart. 1950.

Lorde, Audre. 1984. *Sister Outsider*. Freedom, CA: Crossing Press.

Morgan, Robin. 1978. *Going Too Far: The Personal Chronicle of a Feminist*. New York: Vintage Books.

Oakley, Ann. 1981. *Subject Women*. New York: Pantheon Books.

_____1974. *The Sociology of Housework*. New York: Pantheon Books

Olsen, Tillie. 1978. *Silences*. New York: Laurel.

Reed, Evelyn. 1971. *Problems of Women's Liberation: A Marxist Approach*. New York: Pathfinder Press.

Sobre El Pleno Ejercicio de la Igualdad de la Mujer: Tesis y Resolución. 1976. Editado por el Departamento de Orientación Revolucionaria del Comité Central del Partido Comunista de Cuba, la Habana. In Margaret Randall's *Women in Cuba: Twenty Years Later*. New York: Smyrna Press, 1981.

Zetkin, Clara. 1966. My Recollections of Lenin. In *The Emancipation of Women: From the Writings of V. I. Lenin*. New York: International Publishers. 95-123.

Illustrations

All photographs and artwork are by the author, with the exception of the portrait on the back cover by Fay Henderson.

ISBN 142514044-0

Printed in Great Britain
by Amazon